THRIVE WITH JESUS

A BIBLE WORKBOOK

THRIVE WITH JESUS

A BIBLE WORKBOOK

Lessons in Scripture to Deepen Your Faith

BRITTANY SMIGIELSKI

Z FAITH • NEW YORK

Z Faith
An imprint of Zeitgeist™
A division of Penguin Random House LLC
1745 Broadway, New York, NY 10019
zeitgeistpublishing.com
penguinrandomhouse.com

ISBN: 9798217151097
Ebook ISBN: 9798217331079

Printed in the United States of America
1st Printing

Illustrations © by Shutterstock.com/Great Bergens
Book design by Emma Hall
Author photograph © by Monnette Co. Photography LLC
Edited by Caroline Lee

The authorized representative in the EU for product safety and compliance is Penguin Random House Ireland, Morrison Chambers, 32 Nassau Street, Dublin D02 YH68, Ireland.
https://eu-contact.penguin.ie

To anyone who is looking for Jesus;
come and see that the Lord is good.

Contents

A FORGIVING JESUS

AN OBEDIENT JESUS

A HUMBLE JESUS

A HUMAN JESUS

INTRODUCTION

Hi, friend! I'm so excited for you to dive into *Thrive with Jesus: A Bible Workbook: Lessons in Scripture and Faith*. The beautiful truth about Jesus is that he desires to be with you whether you heard about him for the first time today or you've been following him your entire life. This book in your hand is a great first step in deepening your relationship with him. The more you abide with Jesus and learn his character and heart, the more you will become like him and live a life that reflects your closeness to him.

Jesus is the center of it all. In the gospel of John, he says, "I am the way, and the truth, and the life. No one comes to the Father except through me" (John 14:6). It is only through him that we get to experience salvation, freedom, and the presence of the Father and Spirit. Jesus is the truth that will anchor and guide you through the storms of life.

This workbook is designed to not only help you study the Bible in greater depth and detail, but to also help you catch a new revelation of Jesus's character and teaching. Inside you'll find worksheets to accompany each theme to help you dive deeper into Scripture and begin to read and interpret the Bible for yourself. This isn't an ordinary devotional. I'm not going to lay out all the answers. This workbook is a tool to help you step into a text that is living and active so that you can learn to see, hear, and consider how God is moving and speaking to you. This isn't a basic Bible study book, either. As you read the Scripture selections you'll not only consider the historical, cultural, and theological implications of a given text; you'll also take time to reflect on what this means for you and your life today.

Above all else, my prayer is that when you are done engaging with this workbook, you will know with clarity and conviction the depth, height, length, and breadth of Jesus's love for you. If you can get that truth to sink in, the rest will follow.

HOW TO USE THIS BOOK

As you get ready to move through the workbook, here's what you can expect to find in each lesson, plus some suggestions for how to get the most out of this book. Whether you are using this individually or as part of a group, this book will require time and attention. I recommend opening this book during your daily quiet time, turning your phone off or placing it in another room, and limiting distractions. The more you give to your study, the more you will get out of it.

THE BASICS

This Bible workbook aims to help you expand your faith through a detailed study and exploration of the text and a willingness to remain curious to what God might be saying about himself, not what you want the text to say. The story of Jesus isn't written on dead pages—it is the inspired Word of God—alive and moving in you and in the world around you. The more time you spend with God in his Word, the more you will know what God says about himself and you. This workbook specifically highlights Scripture around the nature and person of Jesus. He is the cornerstone that all else is based upon as you live out your life as his disciple.

The primary texts we will be using are the four Gospels: Matthew, Mark, Luke, and John. These accounts of the life, death, and resurrection of Jesus are significant because they speak to the validity of Jesus's life on earth. The Gospels were written by four different men across different backgrounds, upbringings, and statuses, yet all confirm each other's accounts about Christ. Each Gospel writer spoke to a particular audience in a particular time and place and focused his Gospel around specific themes:

- Matthew was a Jewish tax collector for Rome. His Gospel focuses on Jesus as Messiah and the fulfillment of the Old Testament prophecies.
- Mark was a companion to the apostles Peter and Paul and is considered to be the first Gospel written. He focuses on Jesus's miracles and his authority as well as the cost of discipleship through suffering.

- Luke was a physician and a Gentile. His Gospel heavily focuses on detailed interactions that Jesus had with the marginalized.
- The Gospel of John speaks to Jesus's divinity and the source of everlasting life.

I have used the English Standard Version translation as my reference for Scripture. Some translations remain as close as they can to the original language while others take more liberties and use modern day vernacular. I chose the ESV translation because it remains closer to the original text, which is important when the goal is to study the Word.

It is not required, but I recommend using a Bible concordance, often found in the back of the Bible. It works like an index, where you can look up keywords and it will provide all references to that word in the Bible. You can do a quick keyword search on sites like biblegateway.com or blueletterbible.com.

KEY FEATURES

Theme

I have chosen ten characteristics of Jesus (though there are many more) for you to explore and discover. As you start to show up regularly to study the Word, you will be creating rhythms of discipline and a relationship with God. Each day, these themes have the chance to take root in your life.

Readings

Each chapter theme includes four lessons for you to read and engage with. Setting times that you commit to will help make a regular habit out of using this workbook. Starting any new practice can be difficult, but this isn't about perfection; it's about practice. Each time you open this book, treat the time as an offering to God and believe that he desires to meet you. Take time to read the reading plans before diving into the worksheets. Keeping the Bible next to you will help you engage with Scripture as you go through the questions.

The Scene

The Scene will help you understand contextually what is happening in the text you're studying. It will contain historical, theological, or cultural insight to help you see the significance and impact of Jesus's life and ministry in the time he lived and the people he interacted with.

Expand

The Expand section offers more clarity into the Scripture reading as it relates to the theme and will anchor you to the text as you study. These Scriptures can be read over and over again and still offer new nuggets of wisdom; that's the power of God's Word! Focus in on one theme at a time and get the most out of it.

Observe

Engaging in the text is key to understanding it. That happens when you remain curious and open. The Observe section offers questions to help you engage more critically with Scripture. These questions may be fill-in-the-blank, open ended, or trivia-style. Use a journal or notebook to jot down your thoughts and answers if you need more space. You can ask many different types of questions of the text as you continue to grow in studying the Word and deepening your faith.

Connect

Each prompt or invitation will help you look at how these characteristics of Jesus challenge you to live out your faith in the modern world. There may be action items for you to engage with or scenarios for you to put into practice that week. Connect will help you take your new understanding of Scripture and apply it to your life in real time.

Prayer

Prayer is one of the greatest entry points into deepening your relationship with Jesus. Each lesson will conclude with a prayer to help orient you throughout the week and guide you back to Jesus. Use the prayer each day or add your own words as the lesson moves you.

A PERSONAL JESUS

LESSON 1
The God Who Feels

READING John 11:1–4; John 11:32–35

The Scene

- Jesus is with his disciples two miles away from the village of Bethany when he receives news from Mary and Martha that his friend Lazarus is sick and dying.
- This is the last miraculous sign Jesus will perform before his death; and this is the final event that enrages the religious leaders to carry out their plot to kill Jesus. Raising Lazarus is the ultimate sign, foreshadowing what Jesus came to do.
- Mary, Martha, and Lazarus are not random people being highlighted in Scripture; they are known friends of Jesus that he has shared meals with, stayed with, and taught many times.

Expand

If Jesus knew that he was going to raise Lazarus from the dead, why would he weep? Jesus arrives and does not rush right to the tomb and shout for Lazarus to come out. No, he waits outside of the city and calls the sisters to himself, knowing they would be grieving, in pain, and angry that he hadn't come when they first asked. John 11:33 says that Jesus saw Mary and all those around her weeping, and he was so moved by their sorrow that he, too, wept. Jesus made it a point to be fully human and not disconnect from human emotion. Jesus did not enter humanity and turn off the human ability to feel pain, sorrow, grief, or despair. He was a God with tear ducts. Jesus did not shame those grieving and demand they believe in his power to resurrect. He stopped, full of emotion and compassion, and wept with them. Jesus's actions show that God is not afraid of our sorrow or despair—he meets us in it.

Observe

1. Reading the text, highlight the other human emotions you see displayed in the story besides grief. Note which characters experience which emotion.

2. Do you feel Mary and Martha's reply to Jesus was warranted? If you were the sisters, what would your reply have been to Jesus when you saw him?

3. In all of the emotions the sisters must have been feeling, they both seem to be open and honest with Jesus. What is his reply to their honesty? What tone or emotion do you think Jesus is speaking with?

4. As you read John 11:1–44, pay attention to the things Jesus says and think about what he is trying to get his disciples and the crowds to understand:

   - What does Jesus do when he learns about Lazarus? Why does he not go to Bethany right away?

   - How does Jesus feel toward this family?

   - How does Jesus reply to the disciples when they are worried for his safety?

   - When Jesus speaks with Martha, what is his reply to her accusation of not coming quickly enough? Note his reply to her statement of faith when they speak about resurrection.

   - Look closely at how Jesus responds to the various people in this story. What emotions does he express toward his disciples, the sisters, Lazarus, and the crowds?

Connect

1. When is the last time you were honest with Jesus about how you were feeling? Do you struggle to be fully open and transparent before God? Why do you think that is?

2. In light of Jesus's response throughout John 11, what do you think he would say to you and the feelings you are carrying right now?

3. If you were to put yourself in this story, what would you have said if you were Martha or Mary?

4. Think of a time when you experienced deep sorrow, grief, or pain. Imagine Jesus is standing before you as he stood before Mary. What does Jesus do with your pain and your grief? Do you think he says anything? Do you think he does anything? Jot it down as you imagine the scenario playing out in your mind.

5. Each morning, take a few minutes to journal or think through one main emotion that you are feeling and invite Jesus to show you how he feels that emotion, too.

Prayer

Jesus, thank you that you feel. You didn't disconnect from the emotions of what it means to be human, and you don't expect me to disconnect either. Instead, you meet me right where I am even if I'm in the messy middle of pain, sorrow, and grief. Thank you that you are just as present in my joy, happiness, and hope. Remind me today that you sit in my feelings with me but don't leave me there. In your name, Amen.

Recap

Raising Lazarus from the dead was not only a foreshadowing of Jesus's death and resurrection, it showed that Jesus was fully human who felt sorrow, pain, and grief. John 11 is a reminder that Jesus doesn't expect you to dismiss your emotions. Jesus comes close and feels it all alongside you.

LESSON 2
A New Name and Identity

READING Matthew 16:13–20

The Scene

- Caesarea Philippi was a hub for pagan worship of Baal, Greek gods, and Caesar. The city was primarily inhabited by the Syrians and the Greeks.
- Since there were fewer Jewish people in this region, the northern borders of Canaan, the crowds following Jesus would have been smaller. This allowed him to have more intimate time to teach and speak to his disciples. Jesus asks them what people are saying about him in a place that knows very little about Jewish belief and customs, which highlights the difference between the God of Israel and the pagan gods.
- The disciples' response revealed opinions they most likely gathered from the crowds regarding the prophets and what they said about the coming Messiah. The Hebrew Bible spoke of the promised deliverer of the Jews as their Messiah throughout their prophecies. The audience would have been familiar with this thought and belief.

Expand

Jesus asks his disciples what was being said about him now that the ministry was becoming more public. He's taught, performed miracles, and traveled across the country. He doesn't ask what the religious people say about him (he knows how they hate and fear him), but instead asks what the everyday people say. As the disciples reply, Jesus takes it a step further and makes the question personal. "But who do you say that I am?" (16:15) Simon speaks up and declares that Jesus is the Messiah! In this moment, Jesus not only gives Simon the new name, "Peter" but also the identity that Peter will carry from that day forward as a disciple. It was the Holy Spirit revealing to Peter the truth about Jesus—allowing him to see Jesus as God's son. Jesus desires to have you know him personally, and through your personal faith gives you a new identity to live out in the world around you as you play your part in ushering in the kingdom of heaven on earth.

Observe

1. Jesus asks, "Who do people say that the Son of ________ is?" Peter's response is, "You are the Christ, the Son of ________." What difference do you notice between Jesus's question and Peter's reply?

____

____

____

2. Peter replies that Jesus is the Son of the living God while standing in a city full of pagan gods that were built by men. What does this contrast show you about the God of Israel and the gods of this city? Consider the words that Peter uses.

____

____

____

____

3. Based on the readings, who are the three prophets that people were believing Jesus could potentially be?

____

____

____

____

4. Jesus responds to Peter by highlighting the name of Peter's father and identifying that it was not a man who revealed these truths to Peter. Who does Jesus say reveals truth?

5. Peter's new identity will be rooted in the growing church. Jesus says Peter holds the keys of the kingdom. What do you think Jesus means by declaring, "the gates of hell shall not prevail against it." Will not prevail against what/whom?

6. Besides Simon receiving the new name "Peter," what qualities, new identity, and new vision did Jesus speak over Peter's life? (Matthew 16:18–19)

Connect

1. As a disciple of Jesus, what is the new identity that Jesus speaks over you? Perhaps you want to use qualities that Jesus lists to Peter or that Peter later gave to the church in 1 Peter 2:9–10. Highlight which quality you most need to remember in your current season of life and why.

2. Write down a truth statement about your identity in Christ somewhere you can see it all week to remind yourself that Jesus knows you personally.

3. Memorize 1 Peter 2:9.

4. If Jesus were to ask you, "Who do you say that I am?" what would you say?

5. What is an identity that the world wants you to take on and live by? What better identity and vision does Jesus offer for your life?

Prayer

Jesus, thank you that you not only give me new life through faith in you, but you give me a new identity through your work on the cross. You tell me that I am loved, chosen, and redeemed. My identity cannot be taken away by anything this world throws at me or any lie of the enemy. Remind me of my identity in you today so I can move with confidence and grace no matter what I am facing. In your name, Amen.

Recap

Jesus not only wants you to know him personally, but he also knows you deeply and intimately. He doesn't want you to simply have opinions about him like the people who thought he might be a prophet. Jesus wants to have your whole life and identity changed by the saving gift of faith through him. As Peter declared through a revelation from the Holy Spirit that Jesus is Lord, you, too, can walk daily in the truth of Jesus's identity and your own.

LESSON 3

CONFRONTING YOUR PAST

READING John 4:1–42; Psalm 103; Psalm 130

The Scene

- Jewish people at the time considered Samaritans ritually unclean because their racial ancestry was mixed with Gentiles (non-Jewish people), which was a forbidden practice. Additionally, Samaritan religious practices were not as devout as the traditional Jewish ones.
- Jews thought that eating or drinking from the same containers as a Samaritan would make them unclean. Yet, Jesus asks a Samaritan woman for a drink.
- The shortest route from Judea to Galilee is through Samaria, but in order to remain clean, many Jewish people would opt for a longer route that avoided going through Samaria.

Expand

John 4:4: "And he *had to* pass through Samaria." Scholars believe that the inclusion of this verse doesn't point to Jesus's travel needs, but more of a divine appointment. His disciples would have insisted they go around Samaria, and yet, Jesus insists that they have to go through it. It is not by mistake that Jesus is at the well at the sixth hour (noon), which would have been the hottest part of the day. All the women of the village would have gathered water in the morning when it was cool. Yet, here is a woman, all alone, gathering water at the most inconvenient time. Why? She has been outcast by her community because of her past. John 4 sets the stage for Jesus to finally reveal himself as the Messiah. He had yet to do this in his ministry, and who does he choose to be the first recipient of the truth? An outcast, a Samaritan, and a woman. It was through Jesus's confrontation of her past, and knowing her personally and deeply that this woman had the faith to believe and declare that Jesus was the Messiah, the Christ.

Observe

1. As you read John 4:1–42, pay close attention to how Jesus engages with the Samaritan woman and note any observations around their interaction. Write down any other questions that come up or things you notice.

- What sort of questions or statements does Jesus make?

- What tone do you suspect the woman had when answering Jesus? Why do you believe her tone would be that way?

- Jesus shares the truth about God's character with the woman, but she doesn't believe until Jesus brings this up: ________. (John 4:14)

2. What is the woman's response to Jesus laying out all of her past sins and mistakes? (John 4:19)

3. Jesus reveals that he is the Messiah. What does her behavior tell you about how she received this news? (John 4:28–29)

4. How do the people in this city react to her faith and her testimony? (John 4:30, 4:39–42)

5. Where else in Scripture does Jesus talk about being a fountain of living water or the way to salvation? Find three more passages by using a concordance in the back of your Bible, a basic keyword search in a Bible app, or a search engine.

   - Passage 1:
   - Passage 2:
   - Passage 3:

6. Psalm 103 and Psalm 130 highlight redemptive and forgiving qualities of God. What do these Psalms say about how often and how much God can forgive?

Connect

1. Jesus had to meet this woman so he could speak to her personally about how she was living, what she had done, and what she was facing. Where do you sense Jesus speaking into your life? Do you believe Jesus knows you deeply and personally? In what areas could you open up to let him know you more?

2. Jesus invited the woman to look at her past, instead of her shame, in light of the truth of him being the Messiah. Do you still see your past through shame, or do you see your past through the forgiveness of Jesus? Spend time writing down any areas where you still feel you are caught in shame.

3. Jesus personally pursues you and would walk any direction to find you. Take a few minutes each day this week to look to the spaces where Jesus is pursuing you.

Prayer

Jesus, thank you that you know me personally and are not afraid or put off by my mistakes and my mess. All that I've gone through is my testimony and it can bring many to know you. This week, help me to see my sin and repent so that I can live in the freedom that you give as my Christ and my Savior. In your name, Amen.

Recap

Jesus does not only personally know you, but he personally pursues you. He meets you where you are but always invites you to more. Jesus extends his arm to you each day to come, taste, and see God's goodness. He is a personal Savior that has great plans for your life.

LESSON 4

Jesus Came for You

READING John 3:16–17; John 10:1–21

The Scene

- Jesus says the famous words found in John 3:16–17 during the evening meeting he has with the Pharisee, Nicodemus. Nicodemus is trying to understand who Jesus is in light of all that Jesus had done and taught thus far.
- John 3:16 is a response to verse 15 that speaks about eternal life. "For" connects verse 16 to verse 15 as a response.
- The gospel of John contains seven "I am" statements from Jesus. Examples: "I am the light of the world." "I am the Good Shepherd." "I am the bread of life."
- The number seven in Scripture is considered to represent wholeness, completion, spiritual completion, or perfection.

Expand

Although the gospel appears simple, so much so that this verse is one people reference on the poster boards they hold up at sporting events, it is deeply personal and eternally life-altering. Jesus cares for you, came in human form for you, and guides and leads you in deeply personal ways. Day in and day out, Jesus wants to speak to you and guide you as a good shepherd cares for and tends his flock. Jesus says that those who allow him to lead and personally know him trust the sound of his voice. Even if you don't know what is coming around the corner, you follow his lead because his voice is trustworthy, calming, peaceful, and one that you know well. Jesus came into the world to redeem you, not condemn you; to care for you and not to harm you.

Observe

1. Exploring the book of John, find the seven "I am" statements that Jesus makes about himself.

2. What do these statements tell you or make you think about Jesus's character in relationship to you?

3. In John 10:1–21, Jesus compares himself to a good shepherd. Use the text to compare and contrast what Jesus says about himself as a good shepherd to the other sort of people he mentions. Pull out key details as to what makes a good shepherd or a bad shepherd. For example: a good shepherd does not leave his sheep alone when trouble comes (verse 12).

4. John 3:16–17 and John 10:1–21 have a key theme in common. Both Scriptures speak to Jesus being the only one able to do what? Highlight key phrases or words from each text that reinforce this truth.

5. Not only does Jesus speak to his saving nature, his personal leadership, and his sacrificial love, he also says that he came to give something here and now. Fill in the blank from John 10:10: "The thief comes only to steal and kill and destroy. I came that ______________________."

Connect

1. If the number seven represents completeness and spiritual wholeness, what do you think it says about Jesus that he gives seven "I am" statements to you in Scripture? Consider Exodus 3:14 as well.

2. What does it mean to you that Jesus is a Good Shepherd? Now that you've studied John 10, are there any areas where you need to surrender to Jesus's leading? Do you have any doubts or fears when it comes to allowing the Good Shepherd to care for you?

3. If you were to rewrite John 10 to describe how Jesus is the Good Shepherd, what would you say?

4. Memorize John 3:16–17 and write it down in a place where you will be able to see it every day this week.

5. If you could give Jesus another "I am" statement, what would you say Jesus is like? For example: Jesus is the best friend who picks up the phone at 2:00 a.m. when you call.

Prayer

Jesus, you are the only one who saves. You are the only one who stepped into the chaos of this world—not to condemn us, or me, but to bring me life and life abundant. Thank you that you personally know me. You personally lead me. You personally speak to me. Help me to follow your lead and trust in your goodness. In your name, Amen.

Recap

Jesus would have entered into humanity to save it even if you were the only one. Jesus did not come to condemn you but to show you how to live freely and abundantly here and now. He doesn't save you personally for you to hold a free ticket to heaven. He came so that your life right now can be led by his goodness, his love, and his example.

AN ACCESSIBLE JESUS

LESSON 1

Don't Be Afraid to Interrupt

READING Mark 2:1–14; Luke 5:17–26; Ephesians 2:13–18

The Scene

- The Gospels of Mark and Luke both account for the healing of the paralytic man. Mark's Gospel in the first seven chapters aims to answer the question, "Who is Jesus?" whereas Luke's Gospel focuses on the marginalized and outsiders as the key players that surround Jesus.
- News is spreading about his teaching, signs, and wonders, and a crowd gathers both inside and surrounding the modest home; so much so, there is no way in or out of the crowd. Within the crowd are a few of the religious leaders known as the Pharisees and the scribes.
- Jesus was coming back to a home after teaching and speaking in the regions and was still not publicly declaring that he was the Messiah.

Expand

Jesus's life shows that God is accessible to all people. The Gospels of Mark and Luke depict not only the one interruption of the paralytic coming through the roof, but also the interruption of the crowd longing to be taught. Jesus is not bothered, put off, or angry at the interruptions. He had been speaking and teaching in other towns, and yet, even upon his return to Capernaum, the news spreads that he is there. He doesn't shrink back, hide, or tell the people to wait for a better time. He sits and teaches them the Word. He answers questions. He offers not only the forgiveness of sins but physical healing as well. Jesus meets interruptions with grace, mercy, and love.

Observe

1. Compare and contrast Mark and Luke's telling of the story. What details remain the same? Do you notice any differences or omissions from one Gospel to the other?

2. Based on the themes highlighted earlier in the Scene, how does each Gospel writer reinforce that theme in the telling of this story?

3. Insert yourself in the story. Use each character to draw out deeper reflections, questions, or tones that you may have missed. Characters to consider: Jesus, the homeowner, the friends carrying the paralytic man, the Pharisees, the paralytic man himself. Jot down some questions, thoughts, or feelings you would have if you were each of these characters.

4. Observe how the verses in Mark 2 and Luke 5 point to the access that we have to Christ. Think of these questions:

    - What does this story tell you about Jesus's attitude toward interruptions?

    - Perhaps you feel like you are "interrupting" God with your prayers. How does Jesus's response to the boldness of the paralytic's friends make you feel?

5. How would Paul retell this story in a way that highlights our access to Christ? (Ephesians 2:13–18)

6. The friends of this man were desperate to get in front of Jesus. They had never met Jesus but had faith to believe that if their paralytic friend had access to Jesus, he could be healed.

    - What do the Gospels say about the friends' response or reply?

    - What does that make you think about the access you have to Jesus? What is your access based on? Use Ephesians 2 as a guide.

Connect

1. Do your friends and family feel comfortable interrupting you? What is your reaction when your plans or schedule are disrupted? Does Jesus's response in this story challenge you?

2. Name three people who always create space and access for you. How does it feel to know that you can go to them? Now think of three people who you do the same for.

3. Have you ever felt so desperate for Jesus's time and attention that you would have torn the roof off a home to get to him? If not, what makes you feel like you can't have this kind of access to him? If yes, what was the result? How did your faith and confidence grow in response?

Prayer

Jesus, thank you that you never see my need as an interruption to your plan. Instead, you see my faith. You respond to my need with grace, mercy, and love. This week will you increase my belief so that I can come boldly before you, knowing that you are not turned off by my need of you? In your name, Amen.

Recap

Jesus always has time for you. Interruption after interruption, Jesus was accessible to all people. From the Pharisees and scribes to the marginalized and outcast of society, Jesus held space for them all. From the unbelievers to the zealous, all had access to Jesus's ministry and teaching. No matter what season of life you are in or where you are in your faith, your access to Christ does not change. Your access is based on Jesus's work on the cross and not your own strength or merit.

LESSON 2

Welcoming the Wrong Crowd

READING Matthew 9:9–13; Mark 2:13–17; Luke 5:27–32; Revelation 19:9

The Scene

- Matthew (also called Levi) was a Jewish man who worked as a tax collector for Rome. He would have been hated by his own people and considered a traitor. His lifestyle would have been significantly better than the other Jews and he could afford luxuries from Rome that made him an outsider among his own people.
- Matthew most likely heard of Jesus's teaching and miracles and would have been paying attention to this new Rabbi who was in the district he oversaw.
- The Pharisees, who were the Jewish religious leaders, especially despised the tax collectors, considering them ritually unclean people, or sinners, because they did not obey Jewish law. The Pharisees, seeing Jesus reclining at the table with this group, would have said that Jesus was becoming unclean by association. Eating with someone was a sign of social acceptance, and Jewish people didn't eat with sinners.

Expand

Jesus's priorities were not with the religious people, who were concerned with rule, law, and the pious to-do list. Jesus's priority was always with those who needed grace, mercy, and new life. The fact that Jesus called Matthew, a despised tax collector, to become a disciple, shows the lengths that Jesus would go to show the accessibility we have to God. The very man that would have been hated and despised by his own people was chosen and welcomed by Jesus. Not only did Matthew have access to Jesus, but so did the crowd gathered at Matthew's table—other tax collectors, sinners, and those who were outcast by the Jews based on religious custom and rule. Jesus declares that they are the very ones he came for and purposely chose to dine with. Jesus wasn't afraid of the messiness of the worst of humanity, but sat right in the middle of it all, giving access to anyone who wanted to be near him.

Observe

1. In Matthew's account, there is a verse (Matthew 9:13) that Mark and Luke do not include in their Gospels. How does this verse speak to the themes of his Gospel and his audience? Jesus is referencing an Old Testament passage. Look in the footnotes of your Bible for verse 13 and notice the superscript that directs you to the Old Testament passage. What does the inclusion of this verse tell you about the accessibility of Jesus?

2. Jesus's reply to the Pharisees was about the healthy versus the sick. What double meanings do you see in his response? Is Jesus saying the Pharisees are healthy and aren't in need of him? Or is there a deeper meaning Jesus is wanting them to grasp?

3. Jesus's reference to sacrifice isn't only about surrender or giving up of something. It also references the ritual sacrifices that the Pharisees were accustomed to performing as a way to pay for their sins. Jesus says he doesn't desire this type of sacrifice but instead prefers mercy. How does Jesus's act of breaking bread with tax collectors and sinners show his heart?

4. How does Revelation 19:9 describe Christ's coming?

5. The Pharisees were used to finding mercy through an altar of sacrifice, but Jesus extends mercy around a table. How does the imagery of an altar versus a table symbolize who does and does not have access to Jesus?

Connect

1. Jesus still extends "unthinkable" invitations for people to have access to his table. When in your life, if you were honest, have you felt too far gone to be at the table? What words would Jesus use to encourage you so that you could pray and believe that you have access to him?

2. Have you ever been invited to a table where you felt like the outsider? Everyone around you seemed better in some way, shape, or form. Now consider that the God of the universe creates a table where you're the prized guest. How do you receive this invitation from Jesus? What is your attitude in receiving it?

3. Jesus says he desires mercy and not sacrifice. Where have you been trying to earn love and access to Jesus through sacrifice? In what areas do you need to discover new depths of his mercy?

4. Memorize a Scripture that talks about the table of God. One good example is Psalm 23:5. You can use a concordance or quick online keyword search if you need help finding one.

Prayer

Jesus, I am thankful that you invite me to the table regardless of what I've done or haven't done. You give me access to sit with you, recline with you, and relax with you every day. As I go through my week, will you make me more aware of the access I have and to use it? Open my eyes to see people as you see them, remind me of their access to the table, and give me the courage to invite them to it. In your name, Amen.

Recap

Jesus doesn't withhold access to God's kingdom. Jesus says the ones who seem the most lost, the furthest from grace, the least likely to become a believer are the very ones he wants to sit around a table with. The accessibility of Jesus knows no bounds. You can move in confidence as you approach God, knowing that Jesus bought you this access through his death on the cross and the power of the empty tomb.

LESSON 3
HE HEARS YOUR CRY

READING Mark 10:46–52; Luke 18:35–43; 1 John 5:13–15

The Scene

- Jesus's ministry is about to come to a close before the triumphal entry into Jerusalem. The crowds that followed him have increasingly grown in number wherever he went.
- The stories of Jesus's power and ability to heal were so far spread that even those blind and unable to witness these things for themselves were compelled to meet Jesus.
- Jewish people had cultural norms that elevated rabbis and only allowed certain people access to them. Jesus's popularity and respect as a teacher meant that some thought only the right kind of people should have access to him or to speak with him whenever they wanted.

Expand

Bartimaeus was blind and would have been forced into begging in order to survive. He learned that Jesus was passing by from the large crowds moving around him. Large crowds meant a better opportunity for receiving food, water, or spare coins. Yet he doesn't beg for people's generosity; he cries out for the mercy of Jesus. Jesus, surrounded on every side, shoulder to shoulder with his disciples who were trying to keep the "great crowd" under control (Mark 10:43), stops. Even with all the noise, Jesus hears the cry of Bartimaeus and stops so that this man can be brought to him. Out of all the people in the crowd, Jesus gives access to the man everyone else rebuked. Out of a crowd, the voice of one man stopped Jesus.

Observe

1. Both Mark and Luke have an account of Bartimaeus's behavior. What does Mark 10:47–48 and Luke 18:36–39 say Bartimaeus did when he learned that Jesus was passing by? Be specific. Pay attention to the language that he uses.

2. What did Bartimaeus do when the crowds tried to deny him access to Jesus?

3. What does Jesus do in Mark 10:49–52 and again in Luke 18:40–42 when he hears Bartimaeus? There are four actions Jesus takes as he offers access to Bartimaeus.

- Jesus s________.
- Jesus a________.
- Jesus c________.
- Jesus h________.

4. 1 John 5:13–15 says that as you pray you can have confidence in what?

5. What is Bartimaeus's prayer in the story? Focus on the things he is saying and the underlying need he is expressing.

6. In the midst of a great crowd, Jesus gives individual, personal, and specific access to the man everyone else passes by. What does Jesus give Bartimaeus in exchange for his bold display of faith? (Mark 10:52, Luke 18:42)

7. Bartimaeus was born physically blind, and yet it seems like those who could physically see Jesus were spiritually blind. How did the crowd react to Bartimaeus's miraculous healing? (Luke 18:43)

Connect

1. What do you learn from Bartimaeus when it comes to prayer and your access to Jesus?

2. Bartimaeus desperately petitions Jesus to exercise his authority over him and to grant him mercy and salvation. His prayer didn't include a request to see until Jesus asked. How could you reframe your own prayers to sound more like Bartimaeus's request?

3. Memorize 1 John 5:14.

4. Jesus stopped, called, asked, and healed Bartimaeus. Where in your life has Jesus stopped to meet you? What is Jesus calling you to? Is there something Jesus is asking you to be honest about? What area does Jesus want to heal?

5. If Bartimaeus didn't have access to Jesus, how would that change the whole story?

Prayer

Jesus, thank you that you are so accessible, that you actively listen for me to cry out. You turn your face toward me so that you hear every cry, every plea, and every word of praise. Help me pray with the same desperation, boldness, and faith that Bartimaeus prayed with. Build my faith to remember that you stop for me. Every time I call, you stop and come close. Thank you, Jesus. In your name, Amen.

Recap

Jesus was never so consumed with the crowds or his larger ministry that he wasn't accessible to those cast aside by society. It was often the marginalized that he sought out, stopped for, and healed. Throughout the Gospels, Jesus's life continues to speak the heart of God. He has come for the least of these, and no one is too far gone for his love. Everyone has access to Jesus through faith.

LESSON 4

NEVER ABSENT

READING John 14:25–26; John 15:1–11

The Scene

- In John 14–17, Jesus gives his final teachings and "I am" statement about who he is before his death and resurrection.
- Jesus teaches in John 14 and 15 that he must go away, but that even in his absence there will be access to the Father and the Son through the "Helper" (the Spirit) whom he is sending.
- The imagery of the vine and branches is not new but one found throughout the Old Testament. Jesus uses the language of "true vine" in John 15 and in doing so, is putting himself in contrast to Israel. Israel was not the true vine as they did not keep God's sacred promise; Jesus not only kept the covenant with God, he gave life to us, the branches, so that we can bear good fruit.
- The New Testament was originally written in Greek, so it is helpful to look up the deeper meanings of some words. The Greek word for abide in John 15 is *menō,* meaning a permanence and continuous connectedness.

Expand

Jesus shares with his disciples the importance of holding fast to the access that they have in him. He uses imagery familiar to the disciples—from the Old Testament Scriptures of Isaiah 5:1–7, in which God tends to Israel (the vine) but is met with wild grapes and the fruitlessness of the people. Thus, it is not only important that they remain connected to God through Jesus so that they will be able to bear good fruit, but it is also a way that Jesus continues to redeem Israel's story.

Observe

1. How many times does Jesus say, "abide" in John 15:1–11? List the references. If you are using a different translation, you may see other words such as *remain*, *dwell*, or *continue*.

2. The number 10 is considered to signify divine law, testimony, responsibility, and completeness.

   - How can living connected to Jesus be a testimony?

   - In Exodus 20:1–17, there is another significance with the number 10. What is it?

   - How does remaining in Jesus help you to live according to his ways?

   - Is there any responsibility you bear in the world as a disciple abiding in Jesus?

3. What does John 15 say will happen to those who choose to live apart from Jesus?

4. In John 15, what is the evidence Jesus says that shows you are remaining with him?

Connect

1. Jesus says that receiving the access to the kingdom of God is found through him. How does the Father tend to you as a branch of the vine? What sorts of things can you expect? For example, God may want to "prune" your life by asking you to give up or let go of habits or things that are not yielding good fruit.

2. Jesus says he is with you always. This means through every season, circumstance, decision, or doubt—he is there. How does knowing that he never leaves you change the way you see situations in your past or your present?

3. You may not see Jesus physically, but his promise says that if you remain connected to him you will bear fruit in your life. What is one thing you can do this week to help you remember to abide in him?

4. Name a time when you knew you were connected to Jesus and felt his presence in your life.

5. What fruit of the Spirit do you need more of in this season? Consider Galatians 5:22–23.

6. Pick one rhythm to incorporate this week that can bring continued connectedness to Jesus. Examples: Praying the first five minutes of your day or reading your Bible before bed instead of scrolling on your phone.

Prayer

Jesus, thank you for the access I have not only to you but to the Father and the Spirit. When I am connected to you, my life can bear good fruit. Fruit that glorifies you and is a testimony to the world around me. No good thing comes apart from you; let me not fall for counterfeits but find the real thing in you. In your name, Amen.

Recap

Jesus has never left you without access to him. Not only does he promise to always be with you, but he says that with him your life will produce good things. You will find the completeness you are searching for and the strength to uphold his commands by drawing on the nutrients in the vine. The access to Christ produces fruit of the Spirit in you—it's nothing you do through your own power or strength. He does the work as you abide in him.

A COMPASSIONATE JESUS

LESSON 1

A Peaceful Mind

READING Matthew 6:25–34; Matthew 11:28–30; 1 Peter 5:6–7; John 14:27

The Scene

- The Sermon on the Mount is the longest recorded teaching of Jesus in a single setting in Matthew 5–7. Matthew 6 especially highlights connecting themes around wealth, material possessions, and worry.
- The Greek word for casting in 1 Peter 5:7 is *epiripsantes*, meaning to throw out or throw upon something else.
- The Greek word *merimna* means a mental state or condition in which someone is occupied with or dwelling upon something. This Greek word is used in both Matthew 6 and 1 Peter 5 when speaking about anxiety.
- The Greek word for peace in John 14:27 is *eirene*, which means an inner rest, halting of war, a state of order that yields blessing.

Expand

Jesus speaks to what God cares about. Jesus talks about peace and rest multiple times throughout Scripture, not because worry and anxiety are a sin, but because he knows the human condition is inclined toward anxiety. Jesus's compassion flows from the immense value God sees in humanity.

Jesus came so that in this life people would know his peace, a peace that the world cannot give, a peace the world cannot take away. Jesus isn't reprimanding people for being worried, but he is filled with such deep compassion toward them that he reminds them of their worth. He invites them into a better way, the way of bringing the kingdom of heaven here on earth through faith, a way that is connected to his peace and goodness.

Observe

1. Jesus provides solutions and steps that believers can take to not worry. List as many as you can find. Reference Matthew 6:25–34, 1 Peter 5:6–7, and Matthew 11:28–30.

2. Peter was a fisherman before becoming a disciple of Jesus.
   - In 1 Peter 5, he says to do what with your anxiety?
   - Referring back to the meaning of the Greek word *epiripsantes*, what sort of imagery do you think Peter was trying to convey about the work it takes to release your worry?

3. In your own words, summarize what Jesus is saying about worry. Use one or all of the readings together to paint a full picture.

4. Matthew 6 and 1 Peter both use the Greek word *merimna* to speak about anxiety. Reading the Scriptures again, what does Jesus want people to dwell and be occupied by instead?

5. Look at Matthew 11:28–30 and highlight what Jesus is saying about worry. What does worry do to a person? What does the way of Jesus offer and teach instead?

Connect

1. How often do you stop to cast your worries onto God? Go back through the day and consider the times you did (or didn't) give your worry to God.

2. What is the biggest worry you are carrying? Imagine the words of Peter and cast them like a net onto God. What does it look like for God to carry your worry? What happens to your worry when it's placed on God?

3. Memorize a favorite Scripture from the reading.

4. Matthew 11:28–30 shows that an anxious heart needs rest. What sort of rest does Jesus offer you?

5. Jesus says not to worry about tomorrow. If you were to take those words literally, how does it impact how you face the day today? What burdens does it lift and how does your attitude shift?

Prayer

Jesus, thank you that you desire for me to have peace in my body, mind, and spirit. Thank you that your compassion isn't only for me to live at peace, but that you will take my worry upon yourself so that I can live freely. This week I will focus on the day at hand and trust you for the rest. In your name, Amen.

Recap

The compassion of Jesus is seen in your daily moments. God deeply cares for you to live freely, dwelling upon his goodness over your anxiety. Jesus's compassion toward you runs so deep that he is willing to take on your anxiety every time. Through daily surrender and casting, you can pick up the yoke of Jesus, which he promises is light, pray for your daily bread, and move through the world with a soul that is at rest.

LESSON 2

A Gut-Wrenching Love

READING Luke 19:41–44; Matthew 9:35–38; Matthew 15:29–32

The Scene

- Jesus's ministry takes him across cities and villages where crowds of thousands would gather to hear him teach and to be healed. Often for days at a time Jesus would work his way through the crowds so all who came could have an encounter with him.
- The Greek word used for compassion in all three readings is *splagnizomai*, which means being moved in the heart, and the Hebrew word *raḥamim*, which means the womb-compassion of God. This is the compassion a mother feels for the child in her womb.
- The reading from Luke 19:41–44 takes place right after the triumphal entry of Jesus to Jerusalem. This is when the crowds were blessing him as he rode in on a donkey, and they were shouting hosanna, which in Hebrew means "save us, please." The crowds were declaring him as a king.

Expand

All of the readings highlight a moment when Jesus looked out into the crowds or over Jerusalem and was moved with compassion. This compassion is not a surface-level love or pity. The word used indicates that it is a gut-wrenching sort of compassion deep within Jesus. A compassion that feels more like the love, protection, and care a mother has for a child in her womb. A close, connected, and intimate compassion. This is the compassion that fills Jesus when he stares out at the faces of thousands or looks out over the city of God's people. Every part of Jesus moved to action—action to heal, to provide, or to weep. Jesus is moved by the condition of humanity.

Observe

1. Each reading gives a different reason Jesus felt deep compassion for the people he encountered. Highlight the reason in each text.

   - In Matthew 9:35–38, Jesus was filled with compassion for the crowds because ______________________.
   - In Matthew 15:29–32, Jesus was filled with compassion for the people who followed him to the mountainside because ______________________.
   - In Luke 19:41–44, Jesus wept with compassion as he looked over Jerusalem because ______________________.
   - In each reading, Jesus speaks about his compassion. Who does he tell about it? Why do you think he tells them what he is feeling?

     ____

2. The Greek word for compassion can also highlight the Hebrew meaning for the womb-compassion of God. How do you see the depths of a motherly compassion displayed by Jesus in each reading? Things you can consider:

   - What is happening to the people?

     ____

   - What is their spiritual status?

     ____

   - What is the surface-level need and what could be happening beneath the surface?

     ____

   - What emotions are the people in the crowds probably feeling?

     ____

3. The compassion of Jesus moves him to act every single time. List the actions you see Jesus taking in each story. How would you categorize the needs that Jesus is meeting through the actions he takes? Example: spiritual needs, physical needs, etc.

4. In the readings, do you see anyone having to ask, prove, or earn the compassion of Jesus?

5. Find three other Scriptures in the Old or New Testament where God talks about his compassion toward his people or where God calls on his people to show compassion. In these three Scriptures you find highlight this again: What is the action done by God or the action God is calling you to take? Use your Bible concordance and search for *compassion* or do a quick keyword search on sites like biblegateway.com or blueletterbible.com.

Connect

1. Write your own definition of compassion.

2. When was the last time you were deeply moved with compassion? What was going on, who was involved, what did you do?

3. Of the three readings, which story highlighted the compassion of Jesus to you the most and why?

4. Name an area of your life where you need to be reminded that Jesus has deep, gut-level compassion toward you. Example: your ability to parent, your temper, your self-control.

5. Name someone in your life that has shown you compassion. What actions did they take, and how did you receive the compassion they gave you?

6. How often do you pray for the physical, mental, or spiritual needs of others? Pick one area to focus on this week and invite God to grow your compassion to be more like Jesus.

Prayer

Jesus, there are no words that could ever convey how grateful I am that you are compassionate toward me. You are moved by my needs. You are compelled to act when you see me wandering, lost, and spiritually helpless. Your compassion has no bounds or limits. This week give me eyes to see the ways your compassion moves toward me. In your name, Amen.

Recap

The compassion of Jesus is not void of action. Jesus saw and felt the needs of humanity so deeply that he couldn't leave them without food, he couldn't look at their home without weeping. He couldn't stand to be without them. Jesus sees the people lost in brokenness, their confusion, and their unbelief, and he is moved deep within his bones for them. The compassion of Jesus always moves him to act.

LESSON 3

A Willing God

READING Matthew 8:1–4; Matthew 26:6; James 5:11

The Scene

- Leprosy meant isolation. The disease was extremely contagious, and you would have been kicked out of the city if you were a leper. This is why leper colonies would form in regions where outbreaks occurred.
- There were strict laws given to Israel (in the Old Testament) about what people with leprosy had to do. If a priest declared them unclean, not only did they have to leave their family and community, they were not allowed to worship or make sacrifices in the temple.
- Leprosy was seen as a punishment for a person's sin and thought to reflect their spiritual decay. Leprosy was seen not only as a physical contagion but a spiritual contagion as well.
- Matthew 8:1–4 takes place right after Jesus preaches his Sermon on the Mount.

Expand

After Jesus preached the Sermon on the Mount, a man with leprosy found him. With a large crowd, the man would have known not to go near them, as he was an outcast and couldn't risk making anyone else unclean. This man wasn't stirred by faith because of this great sermon (one that he probably didn't get to hear) but by the person of Jesus. He was desperate to find out if Jesus would be compassionate enough to heal him. The man knew, by faith, that Jesus could heal him. He came close enough to kneel before Jesus and in such close contact that Jesus was able to heal him with a touch. Jesus's compassion restored more than the man's physical health—it healed him spiritually.

Observe

1. Anyone who came into close contact with a leper would be labeled unclean or at risk of getting leprosy. What would the disciples' reaction have been to a leper being this close to Jesus? What was Jesus's reaction?

2. Why does Jesus tell the leper to go show his healing to the priests? Consider the laws of the Old Testament (Leviticus 13 and 14) and what being declared unclean meant. What would change for this man when the priests declare him clean?

3. If leprosy was seen as a punishment for sin, what does the compassion Jesus shows to him tell you about the healing and freedom he gives?

4. Matthew 26:6 says that they were in the house of ______. Do you think it could be the same man? Why or why not?

5. The compassion of Jesus not only healed a person physically but restored much more. In the story, what else would be restored to this man? Think about the lifestyle, opportunities, and circumstances that would have changed.

6. In your own words, how do you see James 5:11 applying to this man's situation? What other situations can you think of that would also apply?

7. Anyone who touched the man would have been made unclean. Although Jesus touched the man, he was never made unclean nor did he contract leprosy. In fact, the opposite happened. What does this show you about the nature of God's power and compassion over the things of this world? The leper would not have had physical touch in as many years as he had the disease. What do you think it meant for Jesus to not only heal him, but to reach out his hand to touch him?

Connect

1. Think of an area, place, or community where you feel like an outcast. How would you approach Jesus with the same desperation and faith as this man did? How would you ask for the compassion of Jesus?

2. Memorize James 5:11. Where do you need to remain steadfast and remind yourself that God's compassion and mercy never fail?

3. Who is someone you have labeled "unclean" and have cast out when Jesus wants to restore them and make them clean? This could be a specific person or perhaps a group of people. Why do you think you carry this view or judgment?

4. Do you relate more to the crowd who would have told Jesus to stay away from this man out of fear, judgment, wanting what was "right"? Or do you see yourself in the desperation of the leper who will go against what everyone says to get to Jesus? Be honest. If these were the only two options, where do you most align? Why or why not?

Prayer

Jesus, thank you that your compassion is not bound to laws, rules, or fear. You come close and reach out your hand to touch my wounds. You don't care what the crowds say about who you should love and save. Help me to see the people around me in the same way. Help me to have compassion as you have compassion, that I would be willing when someone asks for help. In your name, Amen.

Recap

The same compassion that fills Jesus lives in you. As you live surrendered and steadfast under the Lord's compassion and mercy, you are empowered to do the same. The world says those people are too lost, too far gone, too this or that. But it's exactly where Jesus stoops down close and reaches out his hand to offer a healing touch. The compassion of Jesus is not bound up in religious rules, legislations, or traditions. The compassion of Jesus is beyond human understanding but not beyond our reach.

LESSON 4

A SAVIOR WHO SEES

READING John 5:1–17

The Scene

- The pool referred to in this passage carried a local legend that when it would bubble, it meant an angel was stirring the waters. If a person who had any ailment or disease was the first to enter the pool when the water was stirred, he or she would be healed.
- The Sabbath, according to the fourth commandment, was a day of rest when they were commanded to cease all work. Not only did the Jewish people observe the Sabbath day, but the religious leaders and elders created additional rules surrounding the Sabbath so that people would not get close enough to breaking the commandment.

Expand

In John 5:6 it says that Jesus saw the man and knew how long he had been there. In his overflowing compassion, Jesus locks eyes with this man and offers healing. Later, in verse 14, Jesus invites the man to see not only the physical healing but that there is something deeper Jesus wants to heal: the man's sin. Jesus doesn't save from a distance, nor is he a Savior who covers humanity's brokenness with a wide blanket of saving. Jesus saves up close. Jesus sees in detail all the ways you feel hurt, wounded, and lost. He sees how long you've sat in your brokenness and continuously comes close to offer his presence and his healing.

Observe

1. Insert yourself into the story. Which character do you relate to? Are you the invalid man needing to be healed? A disciple watching Jesus's miracle? Or maybe even another person sick by the pool? How would you have felt, witnessing this miracle, based on the character you chose?

2. Jesus saw the healing this man needed on multiple levels. Which of John's verses point to the two ways Jesus saw and healed this man?

3. Jesus asks the man if he wants to be healed. What do you notice about the man's reply? How often do you reply to God with your skepticism and doubt instead of faith in him?

4. The invalid man believed more in the superstition of the day than in the promise and power of God. After his healing, how do you think his testimony would have changed to those still at the pool?

5. The Pharisees would rather see the man remain lame than be healed on the Sabbath. They didn't see as Jesus saw. How do you handle moments when people don't see you or your circumstances through eyes of faith?

6. How many displays of compassion from Jesus do you see in John 5:1–17?

   - What does it teach you about having a faith that sees?

   - Where do you notice God may be leading you to see a circumstance or person through his eyes of compassion?

Connect

1. Think of one person who makes you feel seen. If you were to write them a letter to express your gratitude, what would you say?

2. Jesus sees not only the physical needs you have but the emotional and spiritual needs as well. How has Jesus extended this compassion to you? Where do you need to see Jesus's compassion in your current season?

3. Take a few moments to consider whether you've felt seen or unseen by Jesus. This is the space to be honest. Knowing the testimony of the invalid man, what would you remind yourself in this situation? Pray or journal your insights.

4. What is one life application for you today from today's reading? One example could be sharing your story boldly with those who don't believe in God's power.

5. What superstitions or practices of the world do you need to surrender so that the power of God can take deeper root in your life? An example may include using tarot cards or living off of astrology readings.

6. Find a Scripture to memorize that helps you remember that Jesus sees you.

Prayer

Jesus, thank you that you see me. Thank you that you are a Savior that has the power and compassion to heal all parts of my life. Help me to see myself and the world around me as you see it. Help me to trust that you are compassionate and able to come close to save me. In your name, Amen.

Recap

Jesus doesn't only have compassion for the pain you face; he also sees all the details. He sees you even when you think no one is looking, paying attention, or even caring about you. Jesus's compassion sees beyond the outer need—he knows the deeper love, healing, and connection that you need.

A PROTECTIVE JESUS

LESSON 1

A Quiet Healing

READING Mark 7:31–37

The Scene

- Mark is considered the first Gospel to be written and the primary source material for Luke when he wrote his Gospel.
- One of the key themes in the Gospel of Mark, especially chapters 1–8, is addressing the identity of Jesus as the Messiah.
- Throughout the Gospel of Mark, Jesus would repeatedly heal people (in public or private) and then tell them not to tell anyone what he had done.
- The region of the Decapolis where Jesus is traveling is primarily inhabited by Gentiles. These were people who believed in other religions, spirits, and magical thinking and practices of the day but did not believe in the God of Israel.

Expand

Jesus often healed publicly right in the midst of the crowd for everyone to see. But in today's passage, Jesus does something different; he takes the man away from the crowds to heal him privately. Jesus protects the man from the intrusive eyes of the crowd, those looking on him as if his healing is something to gawk at. Jesus puts his focus solely on this man—not what witnessing a miracle would give to the onlookers. Putting his fingers in the man's ears and touching the man's tongue, it's as if Jesus is communicating what he is about to do. "Be opened." The man didn't hear the words Jesus spoke to him, it was quiet as it had always been. But in an instant, he was healed, speaking without an impediment or any indication that he'd never heard or spoken.

Observe

1. Mark is writing so that people would know that Jesus is the true Messiah, the one true God. Consider the theme of Mark's Gospel and how Mark writes of Jesus's identity. How does this story help communicate that identity?

2. If the man couldn't hear, why does Jesus speak the words "Be opened" in the first place? Consider who or what his words were meant for and how it communicates Mark's theme of Jesus's divinity and power.

3. What does the crowd following after Jesus, begging for healing, communicate about the energy, tone, or feeling in the city (which is primarily made up of Gentiles)? How does this impact Jesus's decision to take this man aside from the crowd?

4. Jesus could have healed the man publicly to receive praise, new followers, or adoration; yet he takes the man to a private place to have an intimate moment with him. What are some reasons why you think this happened?

5. Imagine you're this man. Compare and contrast what a public healing would have felt like to you versus the private healing. What would this private moment with Jesus communicate to you about how Jesus felt about you?

Connect

1. Think of a time you felt protected by someone. What sorts of things did they do or say to make you feel safe and protected?

2. Now that you've imagined yourself as this man and what a public healing or private healing would be like, which do you prefer? A public moment with Jesus or a private one?

3. Where have you created space to have private moments of conversation or healing with Jesus in your day-to-day schedule?

4. Jesus spoke words of healing that the man couldn't hear. Often, Jesus speaks and we don't hear him, either. What is an area of your life where you feel Jesus is silent? If you could hear Jesus say anything, what do you think he would say? What would you like him to say?

5. Reflect on your testimony and write down a few ways you've seen Jesus protect you. This could be protection from an injury, broken heart, bad decision, etc.

Prayer

Jesus, you protect my body, mind, and soul. You create space to be with me one-on-one and desire to speak into my brokenness. You don't need crowds to see what you do—my gratitude is enough. Thank you for protecting me in ways I'll never fully see this side of heaven. In your name, Amen.

Recap

Jesus protects the integrity of the people he encounters. He doesn't parade them in front of crowds to boast at his power to heal. Jesus comes close, intimately, and sometimes privately, to heal what feels broken. He speaks life over what others may have mocked us for and used to label us as sinful or defective. Jesus protects the deepest parts of his people.

LESSON 2

YOUR PAST WON'T DEFINE YOU

READING Luke 8:40-56

The Scene

- The number twelve shows up in the Bible many times. Some examples include the 12 tribes of Israel, Jesus calling the 12 disciples, even the 12 baskets of leftover food after feeding the 5,000. The number signifies a completeness, a divine order in regard to God's governance and power.
- Jairus was a well-respected leader at the synagogue and would have been known throughout the city.
- The Jewish law stated that when a woman was bleeding from her monthly cycle or childbirth, she would be unclean for a minimum of seven days (even if she didn't bleed the entire time) and anyone who touched her would be made unclean until evening and everything she sat on would be unclean (Leviticus 15).
- The Jewish people had laws around ritual purity, especially around interacting with the dead, which would make you unclean. If you were ritually unclean, you would be prohibited from participating in religious and communal life.

Expand

Luke's Gospel highlights not only Jesus's power over disease and death but also shows Jesus's love and protectiveness for the lowest of society, often women and children. The woman suffered for 12 years with bleeding and would have had to hide away from everyone so as to not make anyone unclean. She was forbidden from coming into the temple to practice her faith or even be in homes to share meals.

Similarly, the little girl, only 12 years old, would have been considered ritually unclean in death. Jesus healed and resurrected not only their bodies but also their place in community and their ability to practice their faith in the temple along with the other women and children.

Observe

1. Two miraculous stories take place back-to-back in Luke 8. The number 12 is highlighted in both. Given the significance of the number 12 in the Scene, list the ways you see the number 12 showing up in each story.

2. Jesus speaks to both the woman and the little girl. What does he say to each? What sort of language does he use to identify them? Highlight any words that stand out to you.

3. What risk did the woman take in Luke 8:43–48, knowing that if she touched anyone she would make them unclean?

4. Was Jesus upset at being made unclean by the woman? Why did he ask who touched him? Pay attention to Luke 8:46–47.

5. If encountering a dead body meant being made unclean, why do you think Jesus said the little girl was asleep and for her parents to tell no one what happened? How do you see Jesus protecting the girl's reputation and ability to participate in her community?

6. How did Jesus protect the healed one's reputation and lifestyle in each miracle? Consider how their lives would have changed from this point on.

7. In Luke 8:55, Jesus says to feed the little girl food. Why would he make it a point to have the girl eat something? What does it communicate to the people in the house?

Connect

1. The woman suffered for 12 years and had faith to believe one touch from Jesus could heal her. Where have you suffered and lost hope in healing? How does this story stir up new faith in you?

2. Imagine you are Jairus—rushing through a crowd to get Jesus to your dying daughter and you see him stop because someone touched him. How would you feel to see a woman healed but then receive news your daughter died?

3. In your own life, do you feel resentment or anger that you perceive God is protecting others but not you? Perhaps it feels like God is showing up for everyone else but not for you. Spend time asking God what he wants you to know or believe about this. Is there something in your past that makes you feel outcast from the church or body of believers? Use the truth revealed in this story to speak comfort to your soul that nothing is too much for him.

Prayer

Jesus, you care about me and my place in the world. When the world tries to ostracize and exclude, you create miracles and ways forward for me to be a part of your kingdom. You heal the deepest wounds, you guard my story, and you protect my testimony. Show me how to have the faith to reach out for your garment. Give me wisdom to know when to speak in a crowd and when to know moments of faith are just for you and me. In your name, amen.

Recap

Jesus didn't want disease, death, or religious laws to keep this woman or child outcast from their community. He spoke so the crowd would hear that she was made well. He raised the child in private and told the parents to tell no one. He not only restored their physical health but also their spirit. When all seemed hopeless from a human perspective, Jesus showed that his power was greater than earthly limitations.

LESSON 3

NO STONES THROWN

READING John 8:1–11; Romans 8:1–2

The Scene

- Jewish law was strict, and it did say adultery was punishable by stoning. However, the evidence had to be brought by multiple eyewitnesses who could testify to the actual act with stories that fully aligned.
- The woman would have been held in religious police custody, and the situation should have been brought to Jesus privately (as most matters would have been handled). But she was publicly paraded by the religious leaders in public to shame her and Jesus.
- The verb for "caught" is in the perfect tense; it suggests a meaning such as, "taken with her shame upon her" implying that she was found in shameful places and actions.

Expand

The religious leaders would have plotted to catch this woman most likely with spies, a prearranged meeting, and witnesses to her sleeping with a man who was either not her husband or a man that was married. It takes two people to commit adultery, and yet the man is nowhere to be found. The leaders' vindictive nature wasn't only against her but also Jesus. Verse 6 tells us that they did all of this to test Jesus and trap him before the crowds—either Jesus speaks against the law and could be condemned or he agrees to put the woman to death and loses the support of the crowds. They also shamed this woman in the most public way possible and were ready to condemn her to death and stone her inside the temple walls. Jesus protected this woman's life and released her from shame through his forgiveness, grace, and call to sin no more.

Observe

1. In John 8:5, the religious leaders state that the Law of Moses required such a woman to be stoned. The Pharisees were laying a trap for Jesus. However, Jesus replies not by addressing the woman's situation directly but puts the focus on the heart of the Pharisees. What does Jesus say?

2. What did Jesus say when these men demanded an answer from him?

3. Place yourself among the crowd looking onto the scene in the temple. How do you imagine you would have felt or wanted to respond when you saw this incident unfold?

4. As you read John 8:1–11, what does this story tell you about who Jesus is? What does Jesus seem to care more about? What do the Pharisees seem to care about?

5. How does Jesus protect the woman's life and find justice for her? What does Jesus highlight in his question to the Pharisees?

6. Why do you think the Pharisees leave in order from the oldest to the youngest? Consider their attitude, tone, pride, ego, etc.

7. Does the text say Jesus doesn't care about adultery? What is his response to the sin?

Connect

1. Have you ever felt shamed for your choices or your mistakes? What do you think Jesus would say to people who try to continue to shame you?

2. Consider your lifestyle and choices and think about where Jesus may be wanting to set you free and is speaking the same words to you, "Neither do I condemn you; go, and from now on sin no more."

3. What do you think Jesus wrote in the sand?

4. Remember, at the time women were not considered a viable witness for themselves and would have been at the mercy of the men. In the story in John 8, Jesus doesn't demand a witness on her behalf but speaks directly to her. What does Jesus's interaction with the woman teach you about his desire to protect those without power during that time?

5. Are you holding stones to throw at others who have wronged you? What would you need to do to set the stones down?

6. Memorize Romans 8:1.

Prayer

Jesus, thank you that you do not condemn me. Thank you that you don't parade my sin for all to see but kneel down and invite me into freedom. Help me to set down the stones I pick up to throw at others or at myself. I do not live in the condemnation of the world, but in the freedom you give. In your name, Amen.

Recap

Jesus protected this woman from an injustice by men who were only using her to prove a point. Jesus didn't only protect her life, he saw past her sin and protected her humanity and God-given identity even when she didn't. Jesus reminded her of the truth that she was more than this moment. She was forgiven, she could choose a different way. She could decide to live freely and unashamed. Jesus protects the least of these.

LESSON 4
A Holy House

READING Matthew 21:12–17; Mark 11:15–19; Isaiah 56:7

The Scene

- This story is recorded in the Gospels of Matthew, Mark, and Luke.
- The merchants were set up in the outer courts, the only area of the temple where Gentiles were allowed to come and pray.
- Jesus quotes Isaiah's prophecy about the Messiah and God's house being for all nations.
- The needy come to Jesus after the temple cleansing, and Jesus continues his ministry of healing the sick.
- In Matthew's account, the people praise Jesus for healing those who come to him.

Expand

Outside the temple, the cost of animals needed for sacrifices would have been much lower, but the sellers inside the temple were increasing prices to turn a much greater profit. Additionally, they set up shop in the one place where Gentiles (or "the nations" in Mark 11:17) could come and seek God and pray. The religious leaders seem to take no offense at the defilement of the temple by greed and theft, but are outraged at Jesus who came to purify it. Jesus honored God's desire for the temple to be a holy place for seekers, the lost, and the broken.

Observe

1. Compare and contrast the account given in Matthew and Mark. What details do they both highlight? Where are details left out, changed, or expanded upon?

2. When Jesus quotes Isaiah, he is doing more than using Scripture to speak to the holiness of the temple. What is Jesus implying about himself by quoting this prophecy?

3. What do the people do that causes the Pharisees to be indignant? What does Jesus do that makes them fear and hate him?

4. What is the crowd's response to Jesus clearing out the merchants and the buyers from the temple? The crowd was likely made up of both Jews and Gentiles. What would they have learned about Jesus's character and nature?

5. Matthew and Mark both tell of Jesus quoting Scripture in reply to the Pharisees. Besides Isaiah 56, what other Scripture does Jesus quote? Look for the superscript on the verses for reference.

6. Jesus is protecting more than the holiness of the temple. Why is it significant that he mentions it is a house of prayer for all nations?

7. In your own words, how would you retell the story of what Jesus was trying to say and accomplish in the temple?

8. What does this account teach you about the desire Jesus has for everyone to have access to God?

Connect

1. What qualities and priorities should a church have today based on what Jesus protects in this story?

2. Scripture also says that believers are now the living temple of God. If you are the temple of God, how is your life marked by prayer? In what ways can people around you have access to you for encouragement, healing, and hope?

3. How can you prioritize prayer this week?

Prayer

Jesus, may I prioritize the things you do. Let me not take for granted the ability to gather and have access to your church. Give me eyes to see the ways I have overrun your courts with things that keep people from knowing you. Give me a heart to keep your house as a house of prayer. In your name, Amen.

Recap

Jesus deeply cares about the access all people have to seek God and his kingdom. He fiercely protects the holiness and reverence of the temple and the need for people to meet God there. Today, Jesus still fights for his bride, the church. Jesus shows us that having a place of worship is vital for the community of believers.

A FAITHFUL JESUS

LESSON 1

A Completed Mission

READING John 17

The Scene

- This is the final prayer of Jesus before the crucifixion, also known as the "high priestly prayer."
- Jesus gives an account of his earthly ministry over the last three years and prays for himself in verses 1–5, prayers over his disciples in verses 6–19, and closes by praying for the believers that would come later in verses 20–26.
- This is the longest recorded prayer of Jesus in all the Gospels.
- Jesus's prayer focuses on his relationship to the Father, his work on earth, and his relationship to the disciples and the believers who would come.

Expand

Jesus's entire ministry was to do the will of the Father. He knew that to fulfill the will of the Father would require deep surrender, complete obedience, and faith. In this prayer, Jesus lists all the ways he remained faithful to the work and mission set before him throughout his ministry. He asks that the Father remain faithful to the disciples he entrusted to Jesus and to the believers that would come later. Even though he knew that being faithful to this ministry would result in his death, Jesus remained. In the same way, God calls you into ministry with him wherever you are planted, and it will require the same surrender, obedience, and faithfulness that Jesus carried out.

Observe

1. Jesus's prayer lists six things that the Father entrusted to him throughout his ministry. What are the six things that Jesus was faithful to?

2. Jesus's ministry and faithfulness didn't end on the cross. In his prayer, he says that he will give believers four things. What four things does Jesus give to believers through his continued faithfulness?

3. Jesus knew that the faithfulness of the Father toward him wasn't exclusively his. Jesus asks the Father to do four things for his disciples and future believers. What are these four things?

4. Jesus knew that the believers would remain in the world until the final days. What does Jesus specifically pray for concerning believers in the world?

5. Faithfulness isn't just about believing the words of Scripture or the words of the Father. What actions does Jesus live out and practice to demonstrate a faithful life?

6. What is another verse that highlights the relationship between Jesus and the Father (and also the Spirit)? Consider moments such as Jesus's baptism if you need a place to start.

7. This prayer doesn't only highlight the faithfulness of Jesus, it also repeats one key theme about Jesus's relationship to the Father, his relationship to the disciples, and the relationship he hopes believers will have. What is the theme that he continues to pray for?

Connect

1. Choose one verse or small section of Jesus's prayer to memorize. Write it where you'll see it every day.

2. Just as Jesus had a ministry in front of him, what ministry has God placed in front of you in this specific season? Examples could include: parenthood, your chosen field of work, the neighbors you have, etc.

3. Jesus's words in Matthew 28:19–20 calls all believers to the same mission: to spread the Gospel. Do you see it lived out in front of you? How could you become a part of this larger mission? What is one thing you could do this week to move forward in faith?

4. Jesus prays for unity among all believers. Is there any area internally or externally where you have disunity? Spend time praying in your own words for unity or use the words of Jesus from John 17.

Prayer

Jesus, your faithfulness to your ministry, your disciples, and all believers is limitless. Your faithfulness covers each and every one of us even when we don't remain faithful to you. Help me grow in faithfulness this week, living a life surrendered and obedient as you did. In your name, Amen.

Recap

Jesus was fully human and still chose to live each day surrendered and obedient to the will of the Father. He was faithful to the disciples that God entrusted to him and knew that his faithfulness would serve as an example for all who followed him. Jesus's faithfulness was rooted in his surrender, obedience, and love of the Father and of us.

LESSON 2

FAITHFUL TO FIND YOU

READING Luke 15:1–7; Luke 15:8–10

The Scene

- Jesus commonly used parables to teach. Parables are simple stories with heavenly meanings. Jesus used this method to communicate about the character of God and what the kingdom of God is like.
- There are 40+ parables recorded across the Gospels.
- The crowd was a mixed company of tax collectors, sinners, Pharisees, and scribes. Jesus was directing these two parables at the Pharisees and scribes.

Expand

In both of the parables from Luke 15, Jesus highlights the value God puts on finding and saving, "the one." Jesus is speaking to the Pharisees and the scribes who are (once again) angry that Jesus eats and communes with the people they deem as inappropriate, unclean, and unworthy. As the parables unfold, Jesus says that not only is God faithful in going after the lost one, but that all of heaven rejoices at even one being found. The faithfulness of God to redeem knows no limits, socio-economic labels, or societal boundaries. Jesus is faithful in seeking all who are lost.

Observe

1. Choose one of the parables from the two readings to rewrite in your own words. What are the things you choose to highlight? Do any questions come up as you retell the details? What stands out to you the most about the faithfulness of Jesus and how this is received by the crowd?

2. In the parable of the Lost Sheep, the man has to carry his sheep home. What could be some of the reasons he would have to carry the sheep? How could that be an illustration of God's faithfulness to us? What does this speak to you about the faithfulness of God versus your own faithfulness to him?

3. In each parable, when the sheep is returned home and the coin is found, what is the response of both the man and the woman? What action do they take? What is Jesus telling the Pharisees the kingdom of God is like?

4. What was the issue the Pharisees and scribes had with Jesus that led him to share these parables?

5. Luke 15:7 says that heaven rejoices more over the sinner repenting and coming home over the righteous who don't repent. In light of the Pharisees being Jesus's intended audience of these stories, what is he trying to get them to understand?

6. Jesus continues to be faithful to the outsiders, the marginalized, and the ones society deems as the "least of these." What do these parables teach you about the faithfulness of Jesus toward humanity?

7. Where else does Jesus use the imagery of being a shepherd and looking after his sheep?

Connect

1. What modern illustration would Jesus use if he were to retell these parables today?

2. Have you ever been lost or felt lost? What does it feel like to know you were searched for, looked after, and brought back home?

3. What do these parables tell you about Jesus's faithfulness to you?

4. Notice how Jesus highlights the reactions in heaven to the lost being found. Do you believe you carry that same level of conviction and rejoicing when the lost are found?

5. If you were already lost and have been found by Jesus, do you believe this suggests he will only come after you once? What is implied about the faithfulness of Jesus?

6. Find another parable that talks about the lost being found. Consult the other Gospels. If you need help, a keyword search in a Bible app or search engine can be helpful; or consult your concordance in the back of your Bible.

Prayer

Jesus, you are faithful in seeking me out over and over again. Your eyes are always searching for the lost, and you rejoice every time they are found. Open my eyes to look for the lost and hurting that I, too, may rejoice when they are brought back home. In your name, Amen.

Recap

Parables helped the disciples and the crowds listening to understand heavenly ideas through stories they could understand. Jesus was continuously teaching the mysteries of heaven while being faithful to the people around him. These two parables teach us that the kingdom of God is worried about everyone who is lost, and Jesus is eager to look for them and bring them home.

LESSON 3

He Comes Outside

READING Luke 15:11–32; Jeremiah 29:11–12; 1 Thessalonians 5:23–24

The Scene

- Jesus tells the parable of the prodigal son in response to the Pharisees' offense at Jesus welcoming the outcasts of society.
- In the story, the younger son asking for his inheritance before the father had passed would have been as if the son said, "I can't wait around for you to die; give me what I'm owed now."
- The parable says the youngest son ends up hiring himself out to Gentiles and fed their pigs, which would have made him unclean by Jewish law.

Expand

The parable of the prodigal son isn't only about the father's faithfulness to forgive his son and welcome him back home. The father also has to go outside to meet the older brother. Two sons, both prideful and arrogant in their own ways, and a father who is faithful to go to them where they are. The father throws his arms around the youngest after keeping watch for him for months at a time. The father reminds the older brother of his identity and blessing and begs him to let go of his pride and come in and celebrate. Jesus was speaking directly to the Pharisees who stood outside at a distance, because they saw Jesus celebrating people they deemed unworthy and unclean.

Observe

1. Map out the younger son's timeline using the text. Move through the story, marking the different things he says and does. Consider starting with his pride and his desire to go live his life however he wants. Pay attention to the things he says, what he does, and what it would imply about him.

2. Consider the older brother's story. Observe how he reacts to the younger brother's return home in Luke 15:25–30. What is his attitude? What was at the heart of his bitterness?

3. Read the text and focus on the father. Where and how do you see the father being faithful to both of his sons? What does he do? What does he say?

4. Jesus used this parable to speak about the kingdom of God and God's character. How might it have challenged his audience's belief system?

5. Who was Jesus portraying through the younger son? Who was he saying was like the older son? Who is the father?

6. If the Pharisees were represented in the story by the older brother, what was Jesus trying to tell them in the parable by the father pleading with the older brother to come in and join the celebration?

Connect

1. When have you gone through a season of being like the younger son? What did you do? What did you say? What made you believe that running from God was better than trusting the care God has for you in his house?

2. Think of a time you've been prideful or judgmental like the older brother. Have you ever looked at another Christian and thought, "I should have what they have. I've served God longer." How could this parable speak to you about that heart posture?

3. Jesus invites you to also become like the father, welcoming everyone into the celebration of the kingdom of God. In what ways can you grow to become more like the father in the story?

4. Recall a moment when you knew God was faithful to you even if you weren't faithful to him.

5. How does this parable speak to you today? What do you relate to most? Consider rewriting it in your own words.

Prayer

Jesus, thank you that you are faithful to meet me where I am. Whether I'm coming back home after wandering away or being prideful and arrogant and refusing to celebrate the inclusivity of your kingdom, you come to meet me and you invite me in. Help me to respond with a joyful heart. In your name, Amen.

Recap

Jesus is faithful to meet you wherever you are. No matter how far you've been running from him, how long you've been serving him, or how much you know about him, he is faithful to come meet you. Like the father in the story, he extends all that he has to you. He gives you good gifts and never withholds.

LESSON 4

A Prophetic Promise Fulfilled

READING Matthew 1:1–17; Matthew 1:18–25; Matthew 2:1–6; Matthew 2:13–23; Luke 1:26–38; Luke 2:1–7

The Scene

- Only the gospels of Matthew and Luke record the birth of Jesus.
- Prophecy is a message that is divinely inspired and communicated through a prophet—it could contain an encouragement, warning, or prediction about the future. These words are not merely from human speculation or belief but rather, a revelation from God.
- The birth of Jesus recorded in these Gospels are God's promises from the Old Testament writings of Psalms, Isaiah, Micah, Hosea, and Jeremiah brought to life.
- Over 800 years passes between those Old Testament writings and when Jesus was born and fulfilled all that they said.
- Throughout the Old Testament, God made covenants with Abraham and David, promising that through their line the Messiah would come.

Expand

Generation after generation, God never broke his promise with his people. Jesus's very birth is evidence of his faithfulness. God vowed to send one who would bring good news to the poor, set the captives free, and save the people from their sins. Jesus's birth was God putting on flesh and becoming like one of us. Jesus's life is the perfect demonstration of faith. Humanity had no way to uphold the covenant with God through our own abilities or power because no human could live perfectly, so God kept the covenant on our behalf. Through his own faithfulness, humanity was able to be restored to a right relationship with him.

Observe

1. Working your way through the accounts of Jesus's birth, find and highlight the different promises that were fulfilled.

2. These prophecies did not only say that Jesus would come, but they were specific enough to say how and where he would arrive. What details did the predictions give that you see fulfilled in the details of Jesus's birth story?

3. Now that you've found the foretellings that Matthew and Luke are highlighting, go to the original text in the Old Testament and read the Scripture in context (Isaiah 7, Micah 5). What else does this tell you about God's faithfulness to his people?

4. What does the large time span between the Old Testament and the birth of Jesus communicate about the faithfulness of God to his people and to his promises?

5. Using the genealogy of Jesus from Matthew 1, how many generations passed from the promise given to Abraham to when Jesus was finally born?

Connect

1. Why do you think the Gospel writers were sure to include all the prophecies that Jesus's birth fulfilled? What does it mean to you that Jesus's birth is connected to words that God spoke 800 years prior?

2. Jesus's birth proves that God is faithful to his promise even if human logic says too much time has passed. What is a promise you feel you have given up or feel tempted to give up on because too much time has passed?

3. What does the faithfulness of God mean to you?

4. If you were to rewrite the birth of Jesus using your own present day setting, what do you think the birth story would look like? Is Jesus born in a hospital? The back of an Uber? After rewriting the story in your world, what does it speak to you personally about how God chose to come to his people?

5. Jesus entered humanity in God's perfect timing—in that specific year, to those people, in that region, under that government. How does God's deep attention to detail speak to his faithfulness to you in this current place in your life?

Prayer

Jesus, thank you that you are faithful to every promise. You uphold every vow that you've made to me. You were faithful to come to this world so that I would know you, could be loved by you, and could be changed by your life. Help me see your faithfulness more clearly. In your name, Amen.

Recap

The miracle of the birth of Jesus isn't just that he was born to a young, virgin girl. There is also the miracle of the different prophecies fulfilled through this one birth, foretold hundreds of generations prior. Jesus was not only faithful in his life and death, but even in the smallest details of his birth.

A POWERFUL JESUS

LESSON 1

Power to Live

READING Luke 24:1–12; John 20:1–10

The Scene

- Inside the tomb the burial cloths are found, neat and orderly. This speaks to the way they were miraculously removed from Jesus. Grave robbers or thieves would not have stopped to purposefully and neatly unwrap the body and preserve the linens.
- Hebrew tradition says that neatly folding of a napkin indicates, "I'm not done yet" or "I'm coming back." (John 20:7)
- The stone was not rolled away so that Jesus could get out, but so that the disciples could get in to see and witness the truth that Jesus had risen and no one had taken him.
- The tomb was so large the disciples could go inside. Spacious tombs were only purchased by the wealthy, and Joseph of Arimathea, a follower of Jesus, gave his tomb to Jesus to be buried in. There was enough room for the body to be displayed with a small bench for mourners on the side.

Expand

Jesus's resurrection shows the power of God. Jesus not only had the power to raise others, like he did for Lazarus and Jairus's daughter, but he had the power to raise himself. No other human being or god has ever done that. Jesus goes on to say that not only was he raised by the power of God (the Spirit) but that same power and Spirit dwells in all who believe in him. The power of the Spirit within you isn't only to bring you eternal life, but to enable you to live right here, right now, amid the brokenness and death of the world.

Observe

1. Compare and contrast Luke and John's account of the resurrection story. Create a list of details that are either added or omitted to refer back to.

2. Using your list from above, why would Luke include the details he chose and not John? Consider the themes of each Gospel (see pages 9–10) and what aspects of Jesus they each focus on.

3. Jesus's power to overcome death is talked about at length throughout the New Testament. Find three other verses that talk about Jesus's power over sin and death. Use a concordance if you need help getting started.

4. John begins his Gospel by talking about Jesus defeating darkness. John gives the ending away up front. What does Jesus's power over death offer you? Use John 1:5 as a reference.

5. In Romans 8:11, Paul is writing to the Jewish and Gentile Christians living in Rome after Jesus's death and resurrection. What does Paul say is the key difference in how Christians live in the world because of Jesus?

6. The Gospels make a clear point that the burial clothes of Jesus were neat and orderly. What do the grave clothes show you about how Jesus was raised from the dead? Why is it necessary to include these details?

7. By defeating sin and death, what display of power does Jesus show that he has over the enemy?

8. Before Jesus raises Lazarus in John 11:25–26, he says he is what two things? What does each say about the power of Jesus?

Connect

1. What would your life look like if you deeply believed that the power of God lived inside of you? Is there anything keeping you from believing it's real?

2. If Jesus has already defeated sin and death, what hope does that give you, not only for the future but for the way you face each day here and now?

3. Memorize John 1:5

4. Putting yourself in the story of John 20:1–10, do you think your response would be more like Mary, Peter, or John when you reached the tomb? Why?

5. John 20:4 says that the disciples ran to the tomb. They were so deeply compelled by the news of Jesus they rushed to get there. When was a time you were so deeply moved or compelled by the news of the gospel? What was happening in your life?

6. Where have you seen God's power on display in your life? Consider the things God has protected you from, doors he's opened, and ways he's provided.

Prayer

Jesus, your power to defeat death has changed my life forever. Not only does your spirit live in me in this world, but I will live with you forever in the new heaven and the new earth. Thank you that you bless me to live each day with that same power inside me. In your name, Amen.

Recap

Jesus is the only one powerful enough to defeat death. He didn't overpower death only for you to have eternal life. He also gives you the power to live in a new way here and now by empowering you with the same Spirit. The Spirit of the living God dwells in you to help you face anything this world throws at you.

LESSON 2

YOUR STORMS OBEY HIM

READING Matthew 8:23–27; Luke 8:22–25; Romans 1:20; Colossians 1:15–17

The Scene

- In Matthew 8:24, the Greek word for "great storm" is *seismos,* meaning, "violent shaking, earthquake." This indicates that this was a bigger-than-normal storm, something even these experienced fishermen were afraid of.
- Four of the disciples on the boat were fishermen prior to following Jesus and would have been comfortable on the water and navigating small storms.
- The Greek word for "little faith" used by Jesus is *oligopistos.* This does not translate to mean that they had no faith, but infers that their faith was "ineffective, defective, or deficient."
- Paul writes in his letter to the followers of Jesus that lived in Colossae that Jesus's divinity has existed since before creation and that the Son of God was actively involved in the creation of all things.

Expand

From the beginning of time, Jesus has existed. His power is displayed in all creation and in the way creation obeys his commands, submitting to him without question or delay. Jesus was asleep during the violent shaking of the storm, and remained unafraid, because he knew his power and would not allow him to drown in his own creation. As God spoke all things into existence with a word so, too, does Jesus control creation with his voice. Jesus doesn't rebuke the disciples for having no faith but for having faith that still seems to be missing the mark. They are still trying to answer the question for themselves, "Who then is this?" (Luke 8:25)

Observe

1. As you read Matthew 8:23–27 and Luke 8:22–25, see how these verses fulfill Paul's declaration of Jesus's power in Colossians 1:15–17. Think of these questions:
   - What does the story tell you about Jesus's power?
   - Why should the disciples have believed in Jesus's power over the storm?

2. Considering the background of the men on the boat, the identity of Jesus, and the given storm, what are some reasons you think Jesus was asleep? Remember to consider that Jesus was also fully human.

3. The disciples are not rebuked for going to Jesus for help. Why does Jesus say they had little faith?

4. Paul says that Jesus was a part of creating all things. What does Colossians 1:15–17 say about Jesus's power over creation? What is the purpose and response of creation to Jesus's power?

5. If the Greek word for "little faith" means ineffective or defective, how does the story describe the ineffectiveness of the disciples' faith?

6. What claim does Romans 1:20 make about Jesus's power?

7. Based on the lesson's readings, what are you told about the power of Jesus?

8. Where else in Scripture do you see God taking control over water? Hint: go to the Old Testament and check out Genesis and Exodus.

Connect

1. Paul says that Jesus holds all things together through his power. What areas in your life do you need to be reminded of the power of Jesus?

2. What storms are you facing where it feels like Jesus is asleep in the boat? What does "effective" faith look like in your life? How about "little faith"? How does knowing the end of the story change the way you face the storm?

3. Romans 1 says that the power of Jesus is "clearly perceived" in creation—so much so that all who witness it are without excuse. Where have you clearly seen the power of Jesus displayed in your life or the world around you this week? Take time each day to notice where you see his power.

4. The disciples are trying to answer, "Who then is this?" Reflect on Jesus and what you believe about him.

5. If you could hear Jesus say anything to the storm you're facing right now, what would you want him to say? Is it different from what you think he'd say?

Prayer

Jesus, thank you that you are so aware of your power and identity that the storms don't faze you. You aren't afraid or thrown off by the violent shaking that life throws at me. You stand in power and say, "Peace, be still." I trust you to calm the storms of my life in the same way. In your name, Amen.

Recap

Jesus created all things for himself, through himself, and holds every single thing together. His power knows no bounds. Jesus knew the divine nature he carried, the authority given to him by the Father, and trusted in that power so much that he slept during the storm. Jesus is never worried about storms overpowering him for he created all things on earth. In the same way, Jesus sees you in the storms and stands above them. He rests in his power over your life and is with you.

LESSON 3

Your Fear's Biggest Foe

READING Luke 24:36–39; John 20:19–23

The Scene

- The Hebrew word for peace is "Shalom." It is more than just the English definition of an absence of conflict. Shalom speaks to a positive blessing that comes with being in God's favor. It can also signify that all is well in someone's life because of their relationship with God.
- The disciples witnessed their teacher, Jesus, being murdered and were afraid the same would happen to them. So they locked themselves away, probably trying to decide what to do next. It was in this locked room and state of fear that Jesus appears to them.

Expand

When we read stories in the Bible, it's easy to forget they happened to these men and women for the first time, in real time. The threat against the disciples was real. The Jewish leaders had their Rabbi murdered by Rome. The possibility that they could be next wasn't far-fetched. The fear would have been palpable.

Yet, throughout the New Testament after Jesus was resurrected and throughout his time with his followers, he continued to point them to peace. He greeted them with words of comfort—"Shalom"—don't be afraid. These men and women, once gripped by fear, went on to change the world and spread the gospel. Many were martyred, and the very thing they once feared no longer kept them behind closed doors.

Observe

1. Place yourself in the story of Luke 24 and John 20. You experience the worst day of your life seeing the leaders succeed in getting Jesus arrested and crucified. Judas, who you thought you knew, betrayed Jesus and served him up to the enemy. What sort of fears would you be facing? What would your concerns and anxieties be?

2. What question does Jesus ask in Luke 24:38? Why do you think he asks this?

3. Read the responses of Jesus in Luke 24:44–49 and John 20:22. What does he say to the disciples and do for them?

4. John 14:1, 14:27 and 1 John 4:18 reinforce the peace that Jesus gives to his followers. What does each verse teach you about the power Jesus has over fear?

5. In each of the readings, Jesus explains that his peace is different. How does Jesus prove his peace is enough and can be trusted? What points does Jesus make about the peace he gives and his power?

6. 1 John 4:18 isn't speaking only about immediate fears, but points to the hope that believers have for what moment? What does the power of Jesus, love of God, and belief in that love do for you?

Connect

1. Jesus doesn't reprimand the disciples for being afraid, nor does he do that to you. Instead, he offers the invitation of peace. Where do you need to hear Shalom in your life? Take a few minutes and imagine Jesus standing in your room and speaking these words of peace. How does it change the way you see your situation or your fear?

2. Jesus gave his disciples the true peace of the Spirit and then immediately sent them out into the world to spread the gospel. The peace of God empowers you. Where in your life is God empowering you to overcome fear and step out in faith?

3. God's perfect love gives you the confidence for today and the future hope that God's judgment toward you is kind. Where can you extend the peace of God to the world and people around you? Who is someone you know that could use a prayer for peace?

Prayer

Jesus, thank you that when you speak peace, it's a promise. You are the Prince of peace, and you give it freely to me. Thank you that, as I abide in you, the fruit of peace is produced in my life. Not because of anything I do, but because of your power and goodness. In your name, Amen.

Recap

Jesus's presence, his peace, and his love are more powerful than fear. Nothing can overcome Jesus. Jesus reminds you over and over through Scripture that his peace is better and greater than the peace the world tries to offer. True peace is only found through the power of Jesus.

LESSON 4

THE WORDS YOU SPEAK MATTER

READING Matthew 4:1–11; John 1:1–4; Ephesians 6:16–17

The Scene

- Jesus was tested in the wilderness for forty days and forty nights. The number forty is significant in Israel's story, as seen with Noah and the flood and Israel wandering in the desert.
- John 1 is referencing, "the Word" which both Jews and Greeks would have understood. Jews often referred to God himself as "the word of God" and Greeks understood "the Word" (*Logos*) as the ultimate reason and power that brought perfect order to the chaos of the world.
- Paul describes the Christian life like a solider in battle and all the elements needed to stand firm in the world. The weapon of choice is the sword of truth, which is the Word of God.

Expand

As you read about the temptation of Jesus, pay attention to how Jesus defended and resisted the devil. He experienced the 40 days and nights as fully human. He used the power of the Word of God, "It is written . . ." to resist the enemy. Jesus did not give new revelations or use his divine power as the Son of God to drive the devil away through some miraculous sign. Jesus is showing all believers that it is possible to resist the devil, and it comes through understanding the power of the Word of God. John opens his Gospel by saying that Jesus, the embodiment of the Word of God, has existed from the beginning.

Observe

1. John's Gospel doesn't begin with the birth of Jesus but points back even further to the origin of Christ. What point is John making about Jesus's power and identity as God in John 1:1–4? Pay attention to the multiple statements John makes about "the Word."

2. Jesus uses the Word of God to resist temptation. Look at Matthew 4:4, 7, 10. What Scriptures does he quote to combat the devil? Look up the original context as well by following the superscript in your Bible to the Old Testament verse listed.

3. Jesus had been fasting for 40 days and nights. He was fully human. What would he likely have felt physically when he was tempted?

4. What are the elements needed to defend yourself against the enemy? (See Ephesians 6.)

5. Through the power of his Word Jesus commands Satan to leave. When Jesus says, "Be gone, Satan!" What does the devil do?

Connect

1. Jesus would have been physically and mentally exhausted, almost to the point of starvation when he was tempted. Yet, he was spiritually strong as he resisted the enemy with the Word of God. How do you usually resist temptation? How does your physical condition impact your decisions and obedience?

2. What Scripture could you use in your current season to help you resist temptation? Write it down or memorize it. Example: James 5:16 reminds you that your prayers have power and prayer can help you resist temptation.

3. The power of Jesus's words not only made the enemy flee but sustains him through the grueling wilderness. What words of Jesus have sustained you through a hard or cruel season?

4. The power of the Word of God changes everything. What words of life and power can you speak over someone today?

5. Take stock of the words you speak this week. Do you speak with the power of God to uplift and edify, or do you tend to tear down, complain, or gossip?

Prayer

Jesus, your words have the power to bring me life, freedom, and the strength to resist the devil. This week, let my words be filled with your power. Help me love and memorize your Word so that I, too, can have the power to resist the enemy. In your name, Amen.

Recap

Jesus is the very Word himself, bringing order to chaos, creating and speaking life. Jesus speaks with power because he knows the Word of God is active and sharp as a sword to defend you from storms and cut away at sin. The words Jesus speaks over you are not merely phrases but hold the power of life.

A FORGIVING JESUS

LESSON 1

Restores What You Broke

READING John 13:36–38; John 18:15–18; John 18:25–27; John 21:15–19

The Scene

- Jesus tells Peter that the time will come when Peter will deny him three times, and the crow of the rooster would be the sign.
- Jesus gave Simon the new name of Peter during his ministry. Peter means "the rock."
- Jesus refers to himself multiple times as a Shepherd and as the one who tends and cares for the flock (humanity), and those who believe will follow the Shepherd and his leading.
- John 21 takes place after the resurrection of Jesus when he appears to the disciples on the beach after they were out fishing.

Expand

Peter was one of the first disciples called to follow Jesus and was often the outspoken, abrasive, hothead of the group. He was determined that he would never deny Jesus and goes so far as to say that he would die for Jesus before that happens. Yet Peter, in his humanity and fear, denies Jesus. Jesus came to Peter, finding him right back on the shores fishing, just as he did when he called Peter to follow him the first time. He extended Peter forgiveness, without berating him or calling him out for his sin. Jesus met him with a depth of forgiveness that restored Peter to him and reaffirmed his calling to build the church of Christ. Forgiveness that Jesus gives never takes away but always restores.

Observe

1. Through all the readings, what patterns do you notice? Consider the similarities between Peter's denial and the restoration he receives on the beach. What stands out to you? What happens in each situation?

2. When Jesus extends forgiveness to Peter on the beach, what name does Jesus call him? What was Jesus trying to show Peter about himself and the depths of the forgiveness he was offering?

3. What previous invitation had Jesus extended to Peter? See Matthew 4:18–19.

4. What similarities do you notice between the first time Jesus called Simon to follow him and the second call of Peter to follow Jesus?

5. Did Jesus demand Peter explain why he denied him? Was Jesus's forgiveness based on anything Peter did?

6. Jesus taught Peter that he was the Good Shepherd. What was Jesus imparting to Peter and Peter's ministry through this encounter on the beach? What authority is Jesus giving to Peter?

Connect

1. Consider a time someone forgave you when you felt you didn't deserve it. What happened? How did their forgiveness make you feel? Were you able to easily receive it or was it difficult?

2. Jesus not only forgave Peter for denying him but reminded Peter of his calling and identity to shepherd people into the gospel of Jesus. Peter's mistakes didn't disqualify him. Have you ever felt disqualified by your sin? What does this story of forgiveness teach you about the character of Jesus?

3. If you were standing on the beach with Jesus and he was reminding you of his love and forgiveness, what questions do you think he would ask you?

4. Jesus redeems the smallest details through his forgiveness. What little details in your life, which may have felt insignificant, has God reconciled or restored, showing his love for you?

Prayer

Jesus, your forgiveness covers the deepest betrayals and the ugliest parts of me. Thank you for a forgiveness that extends to the smallest of details. Help me to see the depths of your forgiveness. In your name, Amen.

Recap

Jesus offers forgiveness that is freely given, based on his goodness and his love, not qualified by any explanation you have to give. Jesus's forgiveness looks to restore and redeem even the smallest of details to show you the depths of his love for you.

LESSON 2

Forgiving as the Wounds Are Made

READING Luke 22:63–65; Luke 23:32–43; 1 Peter 2:21–25

The Scene

- One reason Jesus was being crucified by the Jewish officials was for blasphemy—in declaring he was the Son of God. The men beating him and mocking him were now blaspheming him, the very thing he was being murdered for.
- The inscription that hung above Jesus on the cross was written in three languages: Greek, Hebrew, and Latin. Those crucified would often have their crime prominently displayed in all languages so everyone who witnessed it would know the sin they committed.
- Crucifixions took place at Golgotha, "the skull," on the road right outside the city walls because Rome wanted as many people as possible to witness the humiliation and dehumanization of those murdered for their crimes.

Expand

The brutality of Jesus's death can be seen in the torture and suffering he endured before the crucifixion, as well as the act itself. From the floggings and physical beatings to being spit upon, mocked, and maliciously attacked, Peter says Jesus endured it all silently. When Jesus did finally open his mouth to speak, it was after they had driven nails into the tender flesh of his hands and his feet, and his words were of forgiveness. He forgave his enemies as the wounds were being made. No apology, repentance, or confession was offered to him. He gave forgiveness freely in the midst of the pain itself. He not only forgave those who sinned against him but also offered it to the man being executed alongside him.

Observe

1. Jesus extends forgiveness to both the Jewish people and the Gentiles. Who are the ones receiving forgiveness in Luke 23:34? What sins had they committed and were being forgiven of?

2. Who was the only one to take accountability for his sin and confess? What did Jesus say and do in light of this man's confession?

3. What does Jesus's forgiveness teach us about the character of God? What does God require from us for him to offer forgiveness?

4. After the man's confession of faith, Jesus extended immediate acceptance into his kingdom. What is Jesus showing you about who is worthy of his forgiveness? See Matthew 6:14–15 and 18:21–35 for other examples.

5. In 1 Peter 2, Peter writes about how Christ endured his suffering. What does Peter say we are now called to do? Based on this instruction to believers, what does it suggest about how we are also to forgive?

6. Jesus freely gave forgiveness to those who didn't ask for it. What was the response (or lack of response) of those that Jesus forgave?

Connect

1. What wound have you been carrying around and who have you been withholding forgiveness from? What does this lesson of Jesus tell you about how you are to forgive?

2. What keeps you from giving forgiveness as quickly as Jesus does?

3. Even when you actively choose to live in opposition to his Word and desire for you, Jesus forgives you. What does his forgiveness mean to you? What response does it draw (or should it draw) out of you?

4. When was the last time you confessed your sin to Jesus and asked for forgiveness?

5. Imagine you're the other criminal, knowing you are receiving the punishment you deserve, and someone extends to you not only forgiveness, but the promise of eternal life in paradise. How would you have felt in the final moments of your life?

Prayer

Jesus, your power to forgive knows no bounds. You forgave the ones who were actively hurting and harming you. Help me to be quick to forgive because I know you have forgiven me all the times I've hurt you. In your name, Amen.

Recap

God's forgiveness is not withheld from anyone who confesses and repents. It is already freely poured out and available to anyone who would turn to him. Jesus's forgiveness sits, waiting for you to receive it. Jesus welcomes you into the kingdom of heaven here and now, just as he welcomed the criminal into paradise.

LESSON 3

You Didn't Have to Ask

READING Matthew 27:32–44; Romans 5:6–8; Isaiah 53:4–6

The Scene

- Jesus's death fulfilled the prophecy Isaiah wrote about him nearly 700 years prior.
- Paul's use of the word *weak* in Romans 6 more closely translates to mean a lack of moral strength or to be ungodly.
- One theme of Romans is that all of humanity are sinners and all are in need of saving.
- Much of the crowd would have been those who made the pilgrimage to Jerusalem for the Passover. The chief priests, scribes, and elders (the highest level of Israel's own "government") were there to mock Jesus.

Expand

Jesus took the sin of all of humanity upon himself on the cross. His death fulfilled the foretellings from hundreds of years before. Through his death and resurrection, Jesus extends the forgiveness of sins to all people who would receive him. Before any of us knew of our need for Christ, he went to the cross to forgive us and create the way back into right relationship with God—something we could never get on our own. On the cross, Jesus died for those who mocked him and put him there, forgiving them through his sacrifice even when they didn't want it, ask for it, or realize their need of it.

Observe

1. What does Paul say in Romans 5:6–8 is the state of all people when Jesus died?

   - We were ______________________. (Verse 6)
   - We are ______________________. (Verse 6)
   - We were still ______________________. (Verse 8)

2. Identify the different characters watching the crucifixion in Matthew. What are the different characters doing or saying?

3. The religious leaders make several statements to mock Jesus. What are they? What part of Jesus's ministry and identity are they taking jabs at?

4. Do you think the religious leaders would have actually believed in Jesus if he did miraculously come down from the cross? Why or why not?

5. The crowd didn't understand that Jesus was saving them by refusing to save himself. His death was the only way they could be free. Jesus's love kept him on the cross. What does this act of love and forgiveness tell you about God's desire and love for all of humanity?

6. Highlight in Isaiah 53 all the ways you see the prophecy fulfilled in the death of Jesus.

7. Forgiveness is a key theme throughout the Bible. Highlight three Scriptures that teach about God's love of and forgiveness for humanity or how God calls us to forgive. Consider Mark 11:25, John 8:11, and Luke 7:48.

Connect

1. List three things you admire about Jesus based on these passages.

2. When was the first time you remember being aware of your need of Jesus and of his forgiveness?

3. Remembering the truth of what Jesus did for you can help stir up fresh faith within you. As you reflect on Jesus's death, what emotions does it stir in you? What does it make you remember or believe about your own forgiveness?

4. Is there a situation in your life or a recurring sin that you know you need to ask Jesus to forgive but haven't? What keeps you from asking?

5. Memorize Romans 5:8

Prayer

Jesus, you forgave the world before the world ever knew it needed it. You forgive me as I sin against you, and you'd do it all over again. Let me live in a way that honors the gift of forgiveness you have given to me. In your name, Amen.

Recap

No one has the strength to bridge the gap between God and humanity. Jesus's death and the forgiveness he gives is so deep and unknowable—he is willing to forgive those who don't even want it! Yet we as humans can have a hard time forgiving even when people ask. God's kingdom is upside down, forgiving us before we even ask or recognize our need for it.

LESSON 4

No Limit on Forgiveness

READING Matthew 18:21–35; Matthew 5:12

The Scene

- The rough equivalent of the servant's debt of ten thousand talents would be approximately $6 billion dollars today. The one who owed a hundred denarii would have to pay roughly $12,000.
- Jesus is teaching the parable in response to the Jewish custom that believed forgiving someone three times was enough to demonstrate a forgiving spirit.
- The parable was full of common customs that the audience would have understood in relation to collecting on a debt, i.e., the selling of the whole family to pay the debt or being imprisoned.

Expand

Peter asks Jesus how often they should forgive sin. Thinking he is going above and beyond the regular custom of three times, Peter offers seven. Jesus turns what they know on its head, saying not only seven times but seventy times seven—essentially as many times as you must. Jesus is teaching what the kingdom of God is like. Those who believe in God will live with a changed heart that extends forgiveness and mercy just as God does, without keeping track or being concerned with how many times forgiveness has been given. Jesus is connecting the insurmountable debt of the parable to the insurmountable debt that humanity could never have repaid. Yet God forgave it through Christ.

Observe

1. In your own words, what is Jesus saying in the parable of the unforgiving servant when it comes to forgiveness?

2. What two sorts of people does Jesus portray in the parable? What are the characteristics of each? What will happen to each of these people groups?

3. What character is God in the parable?

4. Jesus teaches us to pray what words in Matthew 6:12? Why would Jesus include this in the prayer? What does this tell you about humanity's natural ability to forgive?

5. Jesus uses the value of numbers to help quantify the realities he is trying to teach about God's kingdom. What is the number of times Jesus says we are to forgive? Is Jesus saying there is a limit?

6. The wicked servant who leaves the master and imprisons the man who owes him one hundred denarii does what so many of us do. What is the hypocrisy or sin that Jesus is highlighting?

7. Peter's question is one that reveals the heart in many of us. We want to know the bare minimum we must do to be considered righteous. What seems to be Jesus's reply if we are to follow him and live a life like him?

Connect

1. Be honest. Do you withhold forgiveness to people who are difficult to love or who keep messing up? What makes you want to withhold your forgiveness? What does this parable teach you about forgiveness?

2. In the parable, we learn that forgiveness is not based on the ability of the other person giving what you're owed. How does this idea of forgiveness change the way you approach those you need to forgive?

3. Who is someone who has forgiven you when you knew you could never make up for what you had done? How did the forgiveness mend the relationship?

4. Find a verse you can memorize to help you remember to extend forgiveness even when it feels hard or impossible. Consider Luke 11:4, John 8:11, or Mark 11:25.

5. Pray the Lord's prayer every day this week, specifically focusing on Matthew 6:12.

Prayer

Jesus, you do not withhold your forgiveness because I am in need of it too many times. Your forgiveness knows no bounds, and through you alone am I empowered to forgive the same way. I give you my unforgiving heart. In your name, Amen.

Recap

The kingdom of God is filled with believers who understand that they are forgiven beyond measure, and as they grow in faith, they learn to extend that same forgiveness to others. Jesus's life, death, and resurrection speaks to God's abounding forgiveness. Following Jesus requires surrendering to how the world lives and trusting his ways are better.

A HUMBLE JESUS

LESSON 1

A God Who Cleans Feet

READING John 13:1–17

The Scene

- Customarily, because at the time people walked everywhere and usually in sandals, the host would have water for guests to wash their feet upon arrival, not during the meal.
- Non-Jewish servants were usually responsible for the cleansing of feet.
- The act of washing the disciples' feet is a foreshadowing of Jesus also washing away the sins of the world.
- Jesus removing his outer garment is not by accident. It was a strong symbol to show him laying aside his authority to take on the position, work, and posture of a servant as he washes the disciples' feet.

Expand

Jesus showed even more humility in whose feet he chose to wash. John says that the devil had already put betrayal in the heart of Judas; even then, Jesus washed *all* the disciples' feet. His humility extended even to his enemy. If the Savior of the world was humble enough to wash even the feet of his enemy, we, too, are called to be humble and serve all people, no matter our status or theirs.

Observe

1. Verse two says Judas was set to betray Jesus. Jesus knew this and yet responded by doing what?

2. Imagine you are at the table as this event unfolds. What is the feeling in the room? What tension do you think could be lingering? What thoughts would be going through your mind as Jesus kneels before you like a servant washing your feet?

3. Why did Jesus say he needed to wash their feet? He gives a few reasons from verses 8–15.

4. Based on Jesus's treatment of Judas in this story, did the other disciples know that Judas was going to betray Jesus? Did Jesus's behavior toward Judas differ from how he treated the other disciples? What can we learn from that?

5. At that time, people's feet needed to be washed frequently, due to walking dusty roads everywhere. Symbolically, Jesus was showing not just a physical washing but a spiritual washing. What does this symbolize about the frequency with which we need to be cleansed by Christ?

6. What was Jesus speaking about in John 13:10 when he says, "The one who has bathed does not need to wash, except for his feet, but is completely clean"? Consider John 13:8–10 where Jesus parallels washing feet to the forgiveness of sins.

Connect

1. Jesus clearly says that he washed his disciples' feet as an example for us. What is the message we need to take away from this act? Is it physically to wash one another's feet? What other meanings is Jesus teaching?

2. Jesus says that the master and servant are equal in the kingdom. What does this statement mean when it comes to the humility you are to live out?

3. How do you treat those who have betrayed and wronged you? Would you be able to serve them in such a way that no one else in the room would know what they've done?

4. What role does humility play in how you are to love and forgive through Jesus's example?

5. Pray for clarity over a situation or place where God may be asking you to humble yourself and take on the posture of a servant. What steps can you take to prepare yourself for obedience to his calling?

Prayer

Jesus, you deserved crowns, praise, honor, and glory; and yet, you chose to wash the feet of sinful men. You chose to wash me of my sin. Help me have the humility to see that I am no better than my neighbor; instead, I am called to love them through service. In your name, Amen.

Recap

Jesus was humble, even in the face of his enemy. His response to betrayal was service. Jesus chose to take on one of the lowest tasks in his culture to show his followers that the ways of the kingdom of heaven are not the same as the world. Jesus's humility should tear down our pride, because if he wasn't willing to use his status for his own gain, why would we believe any differently?

LESSON 2

The Glory Isn't Yours

READING Philippians 2:1–11; 2 Corinthians 8:9

The Scene

- Paul wrote this letter to the church in Philippi while he was imprisoned in Rome sometime between 60 and 64 AD.
- A key theme of Philippians is the humility of Christ and the believers' call to imitate him through humble service.
- Paul poetically retells of the life and gospel of Christ, summarized in chapter 2, referencing and echoing key texts of the Old Testament from Genesis to Isaiah.

Expand

Jesus has always been. He existed before becoming human and is the eternal Son of the triune God. Jesus "in the form of God" (Philippians 2:6) means he existed in the true and exact nature of God. Yet, the power and glory of God that he had since the beginning was not something he chose to hold on to as he entered creation in human form. He set it aside as the Creator becoming like his creation. There is no greater act or example of humility than this.

Observe

1. Paul outlines the life, ministry, and good news of Jesus in chapter 2. As you follow along in Philippians 2, list the ways that Paul describes Jesus's mindset.

2. What do you think Paul meant when he said that Jesus did not count equality with God as a thing to be grasped? Use the verses that follow to help inform your answer.

3. Jesus was God in full and yet he lowered himself to become human. How do you think the humility of Jesus compares to the humility you see in humanity? Use Philippians 2 as a reference for the ways humans struggle to live humbly.

4. List the ways Paul calls the church of Philippi to act in light of the work and humility of Jesus. (Philippians 2:1–4)

5. Read 2 Corinthians 8:9. What is another way Paul explains the humility of Christ? Jesus exchanged being a King for being a servant. What does this teach believers about how to embrace humility?

6. Paul is not saying that to be humble is to neglect caring for yourself or that you must belittle yourself for the sake of others. But to fulfill the list given in Philippians 2 is to take on the character of Jesus. Meditate on this list and how the power of Jesus can give you a humble heart.

Connect

1. Using Paul's list of character traits in Philippians 2:1–4, where is an area that you need to grow in the humility of Jesus? Consider where you have pursued your own interests above all else.

2. What does it mean to you that Jesus came as a man and was willing to give up his privilege and didn't exploit his power over humanity? What does it tell you about Jesus's love for you and the world?

3. Think of someone you believe is a good example of the humility of Jesus. What are they like? How do they speak? How do they move through the world and see others around them?

4. Memorize 2 Corinthians 8:9.

5. Write out the gospel of Jesus in your own words. Does your version align to the truth found in Philippians 2?

Prayer

Jesus, thank you that you came to show me how to live a life of humility and not hoard power or privilege. You came so that I, too, would know that the greatest glory is found in humble service toward others, just as you came to serve me. In your name, Amen.

Recap

Jesus is the only one who ever had a right to walk around this earth demanding glory, honor, and praise. Jesus, the Lord of lords and King of kings, set all of it aside and took on the flesh of a man and the posture of a servant so that you might know his immense love for you. A love that doesn't manipulate or coerce but is freely given for you to choose to receive. In response to that love, you are called to live humbly as Christ did.

LESSON 3

Wisdom Comes from Humility

READING Proverbs 11:2; Luke 18:9–14

The Scene

- Tax collectors who worked for Rome collected tolls, taxes, and customs from the people and often charged more so they could keep some for themselves.
- Because tax collectors dealt with Gentiles, if the tax collector was Jewish, they would have been considered ritually unclean and unfit to participate in the temple customs and community.
- Pharisees primarily residing in Jerusalem lived by additional laws and boundaries they set so they would not come close to breaking the original law given by God.

Expand

Luke states why Jesus told the parable before the parable even begins. Jesus was addressing those who valued their own righteousness and looked down on others who didn't measure up to manmade standards. Jesus often told parables to put two conflicting ideas or beliefs side by side. Here, he puts self-righteousness against humility. Jesus told the crowd that whoever lives in pride would eventually be humbled by God. But those who know their sin and come before God in repentance will be lifted up. Jesus teaches that God does the exalting and forgiving work and nothing can be done or earned by our own piety.

Observe

1. Parables were designed to compare and contrast the beliefs of the day against what the kingdom of God is like. What does Jesus say about the kingdom of God through this parable? Who is welcomed into the kingdom? What attitude is celebrated in the kingdom? Who is worthy of honor and praise? Who is the only one worthy of being glorified?

2. In Luke 18:11–12, what is the heart of the Pharisee's prayer? What is he essentially saying or declaring to God?

3. In Luke 18:13, what is at the heart of the tax collector's prayer? Pay attention to his posture, behavior, and words.

4. Consider the cultural significance of this parable. Use the context clues given earlier in the Scene to think about what it would have meant to the audience that a tax collector was the character Jesus chose.

5. How does the topic of pride and humility (Proverbs 11:2) connect to what Jesus is teaching in the parable of Luke 18?

Connect

1. It's easy to get caught up in the good things you do for God and slip into prideful thinking and judgment. The tax collector understood his deep need of mercy and that it was fully dependent on God to give. Spend a few minutes confessing and repenting of your pride and ask God to create a humble heart in you.

2. The Pharisees judged others by their actions. Tax collectors were an abomination to them. Who is a group of people or a person that you tend to judge? Could you humble yourself to pray for them?

3. How does this parable speak to you today?

4. Each day try to start with a prayer of humble confession and recognition of your need for God. What changes in your posture or how you see others when you start your day this way?

Prayer

Jesus, I can trust that you will exalt me, honor me, defend me, and justify me. All you ask is that I remain humble to understand and confess my sin, knowing that it is by your grace alone that I am justified. In your name, Amen.

Recap

Jesus teaches you that everyone is the same distance from the cross, and it's the humble in heart who will be forgiven. The works you do mean nothing if you are prideful and think your salvation is because you're good enough. Christ alone saves. Christ alone justifies. The humble will be given the glory of heaven.

LESSON 4

MADE HAPPY BY GOD

READING Matthew 5:1–10; Matthew 11:29

The Scene

- The eight blessings Jesus outlines are known as "beatitudes" and comes from the Latin word "beatus," which means "blessed or made happy."
- "Blessed" in each stanza is not referring to an emotional state of happiness or something that was purely circumstantial, but a deep connectedness and existence based on one's relationship to God.

Expand

Jesus opens his sermon with how his followers are to live in the world. He says that those who want to be made happy or blessed will find it in a humble, surrendered, and obedient life given to God. Jesus flips the world on its head and says it's not the proud, the most successful, or the powerful that enter God's kingdom; it's the ones who know they are desperate for a Savior. It's those who are gentle, meek, and humble in the world and move in God's love and peace. All these beatitudes are lived out as an example to us in Jesus.

Observe

1. All eight beatitudes follow a pattern, "Blessed are . . . for they shall . . ." Highlight or list all eight qualities Jesus gives for those who are blessed. Highlight or list all eight rewards and truths Jesus says they will be given or experience.

2. What theme do you notice about the qualities that Jesus lists?

3. How do you see Jesus fulfilling each of these beatitudes in his life and teachings? What examples or stories come to mind?

4. Why do you think Jesus starts his sermon by talking about what the people of his kingdom would look and act like? What is he communicating to the crowds who are listening and trying to figure out who this Jesus is?

5. In Matthew 11:29, Jesus calls out what two qualities about himself? What beatitudes do these qualities connect to? What does this teach you about Jesus?

6. How are these truth statements about God's kingdom different from the messages we hear from the world? Consider slogans, campaigns, or catch phrases you hear culture living by.

Connect

1. Which beatitude do you need the most help living out? Which one feels the most uncomfortable to you and why?

2. Line by line, consider how you have received the blessing and joy of God in your life.

3. Is there any beatitude that you struggle to believe is true? What circumstances have you gone through that try to make you believe otherwise? How can you use these verses to speak truth to the lies hidden in your mind?

4. Being a disciple of Jesus is the active choice to live counter-culturally to the world. Pride can keep you from living in the true blessing and joy God has shown us through the beatitudes. Where have you been prideful to think you can do it on your own or in your own way and still receive God's blessing?

Prayer

Jesus, I trust that as I humble myself you will give me all I need. To be truly blessed and happy in this world is to live in the humble reality that I am desperate for you and lost without you. In your name, Amen.

Recap

Jesus came, meek and humble. The Creator of the universe did not assert his power, strength, or dominion by demanding that humans honor and glorify him. Jesus showed that God directs the outcome and holds fast to his promises and the earth and everything in it belongs to the Lord.

AN OBEDIENT JESUS

LESSON 1

Even When You Don't Feel It

READING Matthew 26:36–46; Mark 14:32–42; Luke 22:39–46

The Scene

- These three Gospels each record the account of Jesus praying in Gethsemane after the Passover meal before Judas comes and betrays Jesus.
- Hematohidrosis is the medical phenomenon when the body is under extreme physical or emotional stress and sweat blood, as is recorded happening to Jesus in Luke's account.
- The garden of Gethsemane was at the bottom of the Mount of Olives and was a garden used by many Jewish people as a place of prayer. Gethsemane in Hebrew, "Gat Shemanim" translates to "olive press."

Expand

When Jesus prayed for another way to save humanity, it was more than just not feeling up to the task. His sorrow, anxiety, and distress of knowing what was about to come was so severe that he began to sweat blood. This wasn't a stoic prayer of faith but a petition with his whole body, mind, and spirit asking the Father for another way. Yet, all three times he comes with his request and ends his prayer by saying, "Not my will, but yours be done." Jesus grounded his request in his willingness to be obedient, even when everything inside him was desperate for God to provide another way. Jesus was willing to be obedient to the Father, to the very point of death by crucifixion.

Observe

1. The three Gospel accounts hold many details in common. However, there are a few differences in each. Reading each account, highlight what is unique to each Gospel. Note what is said, who it is said by, and what is done.

2. Imagine what Jesus is physically feeling as he prepares to die. Now imagine that every time he comes back, he finds his disciples asleep. Why do you think Jesus asks the questions that he did of the disciples? What does this show you about Jesus's obedience and the disciples' obedience to Jesus's request?

3. What other Scriptures come to mind when reading about Jesus's obedience in this moment and what is to come? Find three other verses in the Old or New Testament that speak to this obedience (consider Luke 6:46, Acts 5:32, Romans 1:5; 6:16, 1 Peter 1:2).

4. In Mark's account, Jesus says, "The spirit indeed is willing, but the flesh is weak" (Mark 12:38). What is Jesus teaching Peter (and you) about obedience through this interaction? Does Jesus say obedience can be found in your own strength?

5. Why does Jesus tell the disciples to pray so that they might not enter into temptation? Both Matthew and Luke's accounts record this.

Connect

1. Have you ever been so desperate for God to move in your life that you relentlessly prayed like Jesus? What was happening in your life, and how did you see or feel God show up?

2. What act of obedience has God been asking of you? Identify where in your life you haven't been living according to God's Word, ignoring or pushing it aside because your emotions haven't aligned?

3. Jesus shows that obedience is not based on "feeling up to it." Often, God asks for obedience, despite how you feel. What does Jesus's prayer in the garden teach you about your own prayer life?

4. Think of a time you were obedient to God even when you didn't feel like it. What fruit did it produce in you? How did that moment or season add to your testimony?

Prayer

Jesus, thank you that you were obedient even when you knew how painful it would be. Your obedience bought my freedom. Help me to be obedient in the small things even when I don't feel it. In your name, Amen.

Recap

Jesus was obedient to the very end. He didn't lie about how he was feeling, but took all of those emotions to the Father in prayer. He understood the truth that God's way is always better. It doesn't mean it's easier or safer, but freedom is always on the other side of obedience.

LESSON 2

The Will of the Father

READING John 5:19–29; John 5:30–47; John 6:35–40

The Scene

- Jesus had just healed the lame man by the pool of Bethesda on the Sabbath. The religious leaders are so angry that they want to kill him, not only because he broke the Sabbath but because he was calling God his Father. John 5:19 begins with Jesus's reply to them.
- Jesus calling God his Father was understood to mean that he was making himself on equal standing with God.
- John 6 highlights that the will of the Father, the work that Jesus was living out in his ministry, was for all people to come to believe and know the Son, even the religious leaders.

Expand

Jesus knows that the crowds are wrestling through who he is, where he has come from, and asking, "Could this truly be the Messiah?" Jesus still remained obedient to teach the truth of his identity as God and submitted to his Father's will, despite being a target of the religious leaders. The truth Jesus spoke was not only countercultural, it was revolutionary. In John 5 and 6, Jesus not only outlines his obedience to the Father, but also talk about the signs and wonders he does while following God's will.

Observe

1. Find and highlight each verse in John 5 and 6 where Jesus speaks about his obedience to the Father.

2. Jesus wasn't only obedient in words but in the things he did. What authority and ministry did the Father entrust to Jesus? Read through the text and write down all the different things Jesus was entrusted to do during his time of ministry.

3. Jesus was asked to heal the sick, set the captives free, and save humanity from their sins. What does the tasks that God gave to Jesus tell us about the character and desire of God? What is Jesus saying God is like?

4. Read John 6:35–40. What does Jesus's obedience do for humanity? Jesus speaks about the will of God and what he desires in the text. If Jesus had chosen to not be obedient to the Father, what would the outcome have been for us?

5. As Jesus lived in obedience to the Father, he created the way to freedom for humanity. What is true for believers when they live in obedience to the Father?

Connect

1. Rewrite John 6:35–40 in your own words. What stands out to you about the Father and the Son? Write down what Jesus's obedience does for you and the rest of the world.

2. In the readings from John 5, Jesus is clear about what will happen to those who do not live in obedience to his words. What are some of the outcomes that will happen if you choose not to be obedient? What happens if you are obedient?

3. Do you struggle to be quick to obey when God speaks? Consider what keeps you from being obedient.

- Are there lies you've believed about God's character? Are there lies of the world that have you living in half-truths? Half-truths such as doing whatever feels good or whatever your emotions want.

Prayer

Jesus, you show me the freedom that waits on the other side of my obedience. You were willing to trust the Father to the greatest depths so that all could find freedom in you. Help me to do the same. In your name, Amen.

Recap

Jesus knew that his ministry came directly from the Father's heart and his desire for humanity. The Son of God was obedient to the Father so that you, too, could know how to live a life of obedience. Through the obedience of Christ, you have seen the heart and character of the Father, a God who desires to bring life, justice, and freedom.

LESSON 3

Even in the Suffering

READING Hebrews 4:14–16; Hebrews 5:5–10; Hebrews 12:1–3

The Scene

- The author of Hebrews has been debated throughout church history, but most scholars agree that the author is unknown.
- The book of Hebrews does not follow the similar genre structures of being a letter like the ones Paul or Peter wrote and is most often said to be best understood as one sermon.
- The theme of Hebrews is about the greatness of Jesus. Hebrews communicates that Christ is above all things from angels, priests, and covenants and because of his greatness and his saving work, believers are encouraged to persevere and hold on to their faith in Christ.

Expand

Jesus was obedient to death, even death on a cross, willing to go the distance even when faced with the brutal reality of the gruesome pain he would endure. Jesus prayed loud prayers with deep cries and tears, as Hebrews 5 says. In spite of his feelings, he chose to do the will of God. Jesus trusted his identity as the beloved Son of God and believed in the divine identity and power that the Father entrusted to him. You can be sure that the One you follow and believe in is a savior in the truest sense. God knows the depths of pain and suffering and what obedience requires. He shows us that we, too, can be obedient despite the pain and difficulty it can cause.

Observe

1. After Jesus completed the will of God and was perfectly obedient, what was the place of honor that God bestowed upon him in heaven? (Hebrews 12:2–3)

2. What does the author of Hebrews (12:1–3; 4:16) say believers need to do when choosing an obedient life? What are the obstacles we face when we are obedient?

3. Obedience is not easy, but what confidence do these Scriptures in Hebrews give to believers?

4. Hebrews 12:3 says to "Consider him," meaning consider the nature and person of Jesus and all he did. What characteristics and truths of Jesus is the author asking believers to think about? How does considering Jesus aid in living an obedient life?

5. Hebrews 12:4 could be taken as a dismissive statement about your struggles; but what do you think the author is trying to put into perspective for Christians?

6. Hebrews 4:14–16 says that Jesus is our high priest in heaven, one who prays for believers, advocates for their faith, well-being, and protection, and speaks to the Father on their behalf. How does this Scripture help you understand the role of Jesus as your high priest?

Connect

1. Memorize Hebrews 12:1–3.

2. When you experience suffering, do you feel you become more or less obedient to God's direction and Word? Why or why not?

3. What other Scripture could you memorize or study to help you grow in obedience? Some ideas are John 14:15, 1 John 5:3, 1 Peter 1:14, Hebrews 12:11.

4. Is there something you know God has been asking you to give up, take in, or let go of that you have yet to do? What would happen if you were obedient? What is the cost of not being obedient?

5. What is one step you can take this week to live a more obedient life to God? Maybe it's a spiritual practice you will do like praying every morning, spending five minutes in silence and solitude, or perhaps confessing to a trusted friend the areas where you haven't been obedient.

Prayer

Jesus, thank you for your willing obedience so I can live free. Give me the same courage to face the hardship of the world through a life surrendered to God. In your name, Amen.

Recap

Jesus is not unaware of suffering or what it means to live obedient to the will of God. He laid out the example through the worst of circumstances so that you, too, might find freedom in a life laid down in obedient surrender.

LESSON 4

A Law-Abiding King

READING Matthew 5:17–20

The Scene

- The Pharisees would continuously ask Jesus questions to try and trap him. Often, they accused Jesus of breaking the law of God.
- Jesus was Jewish. He was born into a Jewish family to Jewish parents who would have kept the traditions and customs of the Jewish people, including the commands to obey Sabbath, go to Jerusalem to offer sacrifices, and more.

Expand

Those who rejected Jesus, especially the religious leaders, couldn't believe Jesus was the Messiah because all they saw was how he wasn't the Messiah they wanted. They assumed the Messiah would look a certain way, talk a certain way, and behave a certain way. They wanted a Savior made in their image. Jesus came to obey and fulfill every part of the law. God designed the law so that through Jesus's perfect life, death, and resurrection all could be saved. When people misunderstand and misuse the law, it becomes oppressive. Jesus was showing people that through the true law of God and being obedient to God's kingdom ways, there is life and freedom.

Observe

1. Jesus is the fulfillment of the Law given in the Old Testament by God. What are some ways that Jesus fulfills God's Law? If you need help, go back to Theme 4, lesson 4 (page 93); Theme 5, lesson 4 (page 115); Theme 7, lesson 3 (page 152) to review prophecies about Jesus.

2. This lesson's reading in Mathew 5 is a part of Jesus's Sermon on the Mount (see page 58 to review). Throughout the sermon, Jesus communicates what God's kingdom is like. How is greatness in the kingdom of heaven different than what his listeners would have expected?

3. If needed, use the readings from previous lessons to name some of the laws and traditions that Jesus obeyed. An example: Jesus going to Jerusalem for festivals and Passover.

4. In his first recorded public sermon, Jesus makes a point to speak about the commands and desires of God and how the kingdom of God is built on these truths. Jesus speaks directly to those who choose to break the commands and those who obey. What does he say about both groups in Matthew 5:19?

Connect

1. Examine your past week and consider the places where you know you weren't obedient to living the way God called you to live. Spend a few moments to confess and repent. How can you invite God into this week to help and strengthen you to be obedient?

2. Find any Scripture to memorize that helps you when you feel tempted or reminds you of the truth and way of life that God has set before you.

3. When you stumble, what does it mean to you that Jesus perfectly fulfilled every law through his life, death, and resurrection? Why does that matter for how you live today?

Prayer

Jesus, thank you that you perfectly kept the law so that I could be in right standing with the Father. Thank you that you empower me to keep the law of God not to oppress me, but that I might find freedom. In your name, Amen.

Recap

Jesus was obedient to every law, down to the smallest of details, so that through his perfect life you, too, might know freedom. Being a disciple of Jesus doesn't mean that there is no law to obey, but instead means that you are given the power and strength and example needed to obey the law of God.

A HUMAN JESUS

LESSON 1
A Hungry Savior

READING Matthew 4:1–4; Luke 4:1–4

The Scene

- The word for temptation in Matthew 4 and Luke 4 means, "to test or to trap." Scripture says that God tests believers and Satan tempts. The same word can be used for both. The motivation is the difference. God tests to refine, mature, and determine a believer's character. Satan tempts to cause believers to fail and sin.
- Jesus did not wander into the wilderness because he was lost but was led there by the Spirit of God. The temptation came after his public baptism and before his ministry officially began.

Expand

Jesus first identifies with sinners in need of baptism during his own baptism (Matthew 3:13–17) and then in the wilderness he identifies with the ways all people are tempted during his own temptation (Matthew 4:1–4, Luke 4:1–4). God leads Jesus into the wilderness to test him and this is where the enemy also comes to try to tempt and trap him. Jesus was able to resist the devil, not only as God but also being fully man. Remember that Scripture says Jesus emptied himself of his equality with God so as to experience every part of humanity (Philippians 2:6). Jesus endured temptation as a man just as any human has. Yet he did not sin. Jesus redeems all parts of humanity's story.

Observe

1. Both Luke and Matthew's accounts of Jesus's temptation note that Jesus fasted for forty days and forty nights. What was the outcome of this fasting according to Scripture? Why is it such an important detail that both authors highlight this?

2. Why does it matter that Jesus was able to resist temptation as fully human? Why is the humanity of Jesus such a key part of how he lived and taught?

3. There are small differences between Matthew 4 and Luke 4. Compare and contrast what the authors say or don't say in each account.

4. Looking over the list you compiled, what is a key difference found in the first verse of each Gospel? Luke not only says Jesus was led by the Spirit into the wilderness but also makes a statement before that. What is it?

5. According to Luke, how was Jesus able to withstand the temptation of the devil even though, in his human form, he was physically depleted?

6. Jesus, in his physical exhaustion and hunger, rebukes the enemy for speaking the Word of God. What is Jesus's reply to the devil's temptation to make stones into bread?

Connect

1. How should Jesus's humanity encourage you as you face tests and temptations in your own life? What does Jesus teach you about combating temptations as they come?

2. What stories in your life can Jesus redeem? Where does Jesus show up to make things new for you?

3. Do you believe the Word of God is powerful enough to see you through whatever you face in life? Why or why not? Ask God to strengthen your belief or uproot any lies you have been believing about his Word and his power.

4. Each morning through prayer, invite the Spirit to fill you and empower you as the Spirit filled Jesus and empowered him.

Prayer

Jesus, thank you that in your physical weakness you remained strong. You show me how the Word of God is powerful that I need your Spirit. Fill me today with your power so that I, too, can resist the devil. In your name, Amen.

Recap

Jesus shows you that even when you are physically depleted, when you are filled with the Holy Spirit you can be spiritually strong. Even in the most difficult and trying of circumstances, the power of God at work in you is more than enough to withstand anything you face. God may lead you to desert places to test you, but he will never leave you or abandon you.

LESSON 2

HE KEEPS THE SCARS

READING Luke 24:36–43; John 20:19–20; John 20:24–29

The Scene

- The Gospel of John's entire message is written so that anyone who heard, and now reads, the account would come to confess Jesus as Lord.
- After Jesus's death, those who believed were scared that the religious leaders would also have them killed for being a disciple of Jesus, so it is of no surprise they would have banded together in locked rooms as they waited to see what would happen.
- Luke's Gospel reveals that there were other followers of Jesus in the room with them when Jesus appeared to them (Luke 24:33).

Expand

Jesus appeared multiple times to his disciples and followers after his resurrection. In this account, John records that Jesus miraculously appears in the locked room, and Luke records that the disciples feared that he was a spirit. Jesus, in turn, invited them all to examine his hands and feet and see the scars that were left by the nails driven into him on the cross. He answered Thomas' need to touch his side where the sword pierced him and placed Thomas' fingers on the scars of his hands and feet. Jesus was making sure that many witnesses gave account to the very human body that he resurrected. Jesus showed his followers the scars of his resurrected body so that they could fully trust that he was who he said he was.

Observe

1. If Jesus was capable of rising from the dead and he possessed the power to miraculously get into locked rooms, he could have miraculously removed any signs of the crucifixion. Why does it matter that Jesus chose to bear the scars on his body?

2. Thomas denied that Jesus rose from the dead because he wasn't in the room to witness what the other disciples saw. He announced what it would take to make him believe. Jesus miraculously appeared again, seemingly all for Thomas. What is it that caused Thomas to declare the Lordship of Jesus?

3. Jesus made a profound statement to Thomas in John 20. What was the statement Jesus made about other believers? Who would be among that category of believers?

4. The resurrected human body of Jesus speaks to the power of God. There is no other religion that has a god that has willingly sacrificed themselves for their followers through death and was then miraculously raised from the dead. Only Jesus has done this. Why would Jesus show his resurrected body to all of these men and women before he ascended into heaven? How does it support the Christian story?

5. What human reactions did the disciples display? What about in Thomas's reaction? How does Jesus respond to each of these reactions and responses? For example, when Thomas doubted and demanded a sign, what did Jesus say or not say to Thomas about his doubt? Consider their interactions and what it communicates.

Connect

1. Thomas is given a bad reputation as being the "doubter," but he was also honest. What is something to be admired about the way Thomas expressed his faith (or lack of one)? How should that encourage you when it comes to being honest with God about what you're feeling?

2. Jesus didn't hide the scars of his past but showed them as the testimony of God's redemptive power. What scars do you carry that are your witness and testimony to the world around you. How do they show what God has brought you through?

3. Jesus said that those who believe without needing to see him would be blessed. How have you been blessed by God this week? Don't overlook the little details and everyday miracles.

Prayer

Jesus, you use the simplest means to prove your divinity and power. You ate food and kept the scars so that your disciples would know the truth that it was really you. Their testimony and witness also help me know it is really you. In your name, Amen.

Recap

Jesus did not ask for food only because he was hungry or wanted to share a meal with his disciples. He used food as a means to prove that he had resurrected as fully human in a human body. Instead of removing the scars and wounds, he kept them to show that he was who he said he was. In that way, his disciples could see the reality and evidence of the resurrection in his human body.

LESSON 3
The Rest You Need

READING Matthew 8:16; Matthew 8:23–24; Mark 6:30–32; Luke 5:15–16

The Scene

- During Jesus's three years of public ministry, crowds would gather from all across the region because they believed in him, needed healing and deliverance, or wanted to witness the miraculous.
- Throughout the Gospels, the authors note the many times Jesus would draw away for days or weeks at a time to be alone and pray.
- The Greek word for "desolate places" in Luke 5 is *erēmos* and can mean, "desert, uninhabited wilderness, remote, and solitary" and is the same word used by Jesus in Mark 6.

Expand

Jesus did not serve and minister to the thousands of people who would surround him purely out of his godliness. The authors of the Gospel take care to note that Jesus frequently was tired, exhausted, and needing to withdraw to be alone in the solitary places to rest. Jesus was fully human and experienced exhaustion as anyone else would. He experienced the overwhelm of crowds and he needed moments alone to be filled up again by the presence of God. His need for space and rest didn't mean that Jesus loved people any less. Jesus taught this rhythm of service and rest to his disciples. God is not interested in building his kingdom on the burnout of believers. Jesus's humanity in his rest shows believers how much more they need rest, too.

Observe

1. What do each of the readings teach you about the humanity of Jesus? What are the authors trying to communicate to the readers about Jesus?

2. Jesus seems to have boundaries and a balance between ministry and rest. He stretches and pushes himself to show up and be available to people. Scripture often alludes to him not eating for hours or days and not sleeping normal hours each night. Yet, the more Jesus gave, the more he would get away to pray and be alone with God. What do these Scriptures, and this trait of Jesus, show you about God's desire for humans to rest?

3. As we think through Jesus's rhythm of work and rest, we see he is showing believers where his strength comes from and how he is empowered to minister. Where is that strength found? Based on how Jesus worked and rested, how should we as believers minister to others? Whose strength are you pulling from and where should you find strength?

4. In Matthew 8, why do you think Jesus fell asleep on the boat? Consider the stories that come before it. What is Matthew telling you about how Jesus gave of himself to the people?

5. What commandment aligns with God's desire for people to rest? Read Exodus 20 if you need help.

Connect

1. How often do you truly rest? What does rest rooted in the presence of God look like for you? When was the last time you got away and was alone with God, undistracted?

2. What rhythms or practices could you create this week as you begin to try to rest with God and find the balance that Jesus exemplifies?

3. What makes you feel like you can't rest? What fears or anxieties come up when you think about stepping away from the world for a real rest or Sabbath with God? What truth would God want to speak into those fears?

4. Rest confronts you with your finite abilities. Where have you been avoiding rest and feeling burned out? How can you prioritize true godly rest this week?

Prayer

Jesus, you show me how to rest. Your humanity teaches me that my humanity is not something to try and override or diminish. Help me to honor my own body's need to rest and recover with you. In your name, Amen.

Recap

Jesus took regular rests and told his disciples to do the same. Jesus did not live untouched by exhaustion or the need to recharge away from people and crowds. His ministry was not built on the back of burnout but on regular rhythms of rest in the presence of the Father and Spirit.

LESSON 4
A Human Savior

READING Isaiah 53:3–6; John 1:14–18; John 14:12–14; Hebrews 2:14–18

The Scene

- Through the humanity of Jesus, he lived in a way that redeemed all the ways that Adam fell short. Throughout the Gospels, the authors point to the parallels of Adam and Jesus. It was Jesus's mission to restore what was lost in Eden not only for Adam, but for all of humankind.
- Through Jesus's death and resurrection, he conquered death. No one has possessed (or possesses) the ability to conquer death besides Jesus. Jesus had to come in human form and go through all of the human experience in order to overcome death's grip on his creation. The power of death has held every other person except Jesus. Death was no match for Jesus's authority.
- Jesus's life on earth is not only recorded in the Bible but also in other historical texts written, for example, by Jewish and Roman historians.

Expand

Jesus is fully God. Full stop. But Scripture and other historical texts make it clear that he was completely human. Jesus suffered, grieved, laughed, cried, ate, danced, and slept. Jesus embodied the entire human experience in his own flesh and blood so that all believers would know that he is trustworthy and a God who understands. Jesus never asks something of his disciples that he has not endured himself. Jesus as God is beautiful. Jesus as human is miraculous. A Savior-God who was willing to suffer at the hands of his creation in order that those very created beings may know real freedom is unprecedented. There is no one like Jesus.

Observe

1. Why does it matter that Jesus performed all the miracles as a human and not simply as God? What promise does Jesus give to his believers about the works they will do? (John 14)

2. Jesus came as the Word of God to restore perfect order to this chaotic world. What does John 1 say about both the divinity and humanity of Jesus?

3. Isaiah foretold how the promised Messiah would be fully human. What picture does Isaiah paint for the type of Savior that God was sending? What would this Savior experience on earth and what would he look like?

4. Hebrews mentions the family of Jesus and how he was made in their likeness. What other Scripture in the Bible talks about someone being made in the likeness of another? Hint: look to the Old Testament in Genesis 1.

5. Hebrews talks about why it mattered that Jesus came and experienced everything that humans go through. What does the author say is the reason for this?

Connect

1. Jesus teaches you a different way to live as a human in the kingdom of God. What does it mean to you personally that Jesus did all that he did on earth as God in flesh, fully human? What do you think God desires for you as you live on the earth in your own skin?

2. Have you ever witnessed the miraculous? Where were you? What happened? If you haven't, do you believe that the miraculous still happens? Why or why not?

3. If the Word of God is true, as you've studied so far, and if Jesus is trustworthy in all that he has said, do you believe him when he says you will do more than he did on this earth? What step would you need to take to live out that belief?

4. Why is it important that your Savior be fully God and fully human?

Prayer

Jesus, I love your humanity, because your humanity shows me how to live as a human in this broken and chaotic world. Your life teaches me how to follow the Father and live in step with the Spirit. Please show me how to live in your power. In your name, Amen.

Recap

Jesus performed every miracle as a human man. He was filled by the Spirit and promises believers that they, too, will do even more than he did. Through the power of the Spirit living in you, you are called to a life of the miraculous because Jesus showed you how to do so through his human experience.

RESOURCES

BOOKS

Brown, Francis, Samuel R. Driver, and Charles A. Briggs. The Brown-Driver-Briggs Hebrew and English Lexicon. 1,232 pp. Peabody, MA: Hendrickson Publishers, 2024.

ESV Study Bible. Wheaton, IL: Crossway, 2008.

NLT Study Bible. Wheaton, IL: Tyndale House, 2008.

Nouwen, Henri J. M. *The Return of the Prodigal Son: A Story of Homecoming*. New York: Doubleday, 1991.

NRSV Study Bible. Grand Rapids, MI: Zondervan, 1990.

Strong, James. *Strong's Exhaustive Concordance of the Bible*. Updated ed. Peabody, MA: Hendrickson Publishers, 2007.

Willard, Dallas. *The Scandal of the Kingdom: How the Parables of Jesus Revolutionize Life with God*. Grand Rapids, MI: Zondervan, 2024.

COMMENTARIES, ARTICLES, AND STUDY TOOLS

Bible Project. bibleproject.com.

Blue Letter Bible. blueletterbible.org.

Guzik, David. *Enduring Word Bible Commentary*. 1996–2025. enduringword.com.

STEP Bible. stepbible.org.

ACKNOWLEDGMENTS

Writing a book seems like a solitary endeavor, but that's far from true. If it wasn't for my incredible community supporting me, I think I'd still be staring at that blinking cursor on my screen.

Kathryn and Carter, thank you for always being willing to mull over themes, texts, and Scriptures with me whenever I needed it, always allowing me to soundboard ideas off of you and graciously listening to me wrestle through the pain points while making sure to celebrate the ideas God gave me as they came, reminding me that there is a well of truth within me. All I had to do was trust God to pour it out.

BG, Leona, and Tabi—you three are some of my biggest cheerleaders. Case and point, as soon as you learned about this project, you were planning release parties and reminding me how far Jesus has brought me to this point in my story. None of you allows me to shrink away from celebration. Thank you.

To the incredible team at Zeitgeist, thank you for entrusting me with this work and valuing my voice and relationship to Jesus. You gave me the space to talk about the Jesus I love and share it with the world. I'm forever grateful.

Finally, to Mom and Dad. Thank you for making sure that I knew Jesus. He's the sweetest friend you've ever introduced me to, and my life is forever and eternally changed. Thank you for loving Jesus and, in turn, showing me that he is so worth loving.

ABOUT THE AUTHOR

BRITTANY SMIGIELSKI is a lifelong Jesus follower who believes in building faith and telling stories, preferably over a cold brew. She is a Midwest girl who calls Brooklyn, New York, home with her dog, Fenway. She has always felt a strong call to ministry since she was a young girl and went on to earn her bachelor's in biblical studies and her master's in religious education and leadership from Rochester Christian University. She is a writer and teacher who aims to help others walk in freedom, grow in discipleship, and love Jesus to the end through her online resources, weekly newsletter, and courses. Brittany works as a spiritual director through her Soul Care Mentorship program, where she walks alongside women from all ages and stages of faith, whether they are seeking deeper formation, a safe place to ask hard questions, accountability, or help through their current season. Find out more at brittanysmigielski.com and connect with Brittany on Instagram @brittanysmigielski.

NOTES

NOTES

Hi there,

We hope you enjoyed *Thrive with Jesus*. If you have any questions or concerns about your book, or have received a damaged copy, please contact customerservice@penguinrandomhouse.com. We're here and happy to help.

Also, please consider writing a review on your favorite retailer's website to let others know what you thought of the book!

Sincerely,

The Zeitgeist Team